SCOTT FORESMAN · ADDISON WESLEY

Mathematics

Grade 5

Problem Solving Masters/Workbook

PEARSON

Scott
Foresman

Editorial Offices: Glenview, Illinois • Parsippany, New Jersey • New York, New York

Sales Offices: Parsippany, New Jersey • Duluth, Georgia • Glenview, Illinois
Coppell, Texas • Ontario, California • Mesa, Arizona

ISBN 0-328-04963-8

3 4 5 6 7 8 9 10 V084 09 08 07 06 05 04

Place Value Through Billions

Five federal government organizations are active in putting out wildfires. The table shows how much money each organization spent during three different years of fighting wildfires.

Money Spent Fighting Wildfires

	1998	2000	2002
Bureau of Land Management	$63,177,000	$180,567,000	$204,666,000
Bureau of Indian Affairs	$27,366,000	$93,042,000	$109,055,000
Fish and Wildlife Service	$3,800,000	$9,417,000	$15,245,000
National Park Service	$19,183,000	$53,341,000	$66,001,000
USDA Forest Service	$215,000,000	$1,026,000,000	$1,266,274,000
Total	$328,526,000	$1,362,367,000	$1,661,334,000

1. What is the value in dollars of the digit in the greatest place for each year's total?

_____

_____

2. Write in short-word form the number of dollars the USDA Forest Service spent on putting out wildfires in the year 2000.

_____

3. Write in expanded form the number of dollars the Fish and Wildlife Service spent on putting out wildfires in 2002.

_____

4. **Writing in Math** Explain why the value of a digit depends on its place value.

_____

_____

Comparing and Ordering Whole Numbers

Show Dogs The American Kennel Club keeps a list of purebred dogs registered by their owners. The table shows the four most popular breeds registered with the club in the years 2000 and 2001.

Dogs Registered with the American Kennel Club

Breed	2000	2001
Dachshunds	54,773	50,478
Yorkshire terriers	43,574	42,025
Beagles	52,026	50,419
Labrador retrievers	172,841	165,970

1. In 2000, which breed of dog had the greatest number registered?

   _____

2. In 2000, which breed of dog had the least number registered?

   _____

3. Order the breeds from the greatest number to the least number registered in 2001.

   _____

   _____

4. **Writing in Math** When comparing two numbers, should you begin comparing the digits from the right or the left? Why?

   _____

   _____

   _____

Place Value Through Thousandths

A men's college swim team keeps records of its best
race times in different lengths of races and swim strokes.
The best time using a freestyle stroke for 50 m is
22.72 sec. The best time using a backstroke for
100 m is 54.04 sec.

1. Write the time of the 50 m freestyle record in word form.

_____

_____

2. Write the time of the 100 m backstroke record in expanded form.

_____

Men's Olympic Swimming Records

Event	Time
100 m freestyle	47.84 seconds
100 m backstroke	53.72 seconds
100 m butterfly	51.96 seconds

3. What is the value of the 8 in the 100 m
freestyle record?   _____

4. What is the place value of the 6 in the
100 m butterfly record?   _____

5. Writing in Math Explain how you write the number 20.158
in word form.

_____

_____

_____

_____

Comparing and Ordering Decimals

Groceries Saraline and her mother went grocery shopping. They bought bread for $2.51, a pineapple for $3.60, a bag of tomatoes for $2.57, and fish for $3.09.

1. Which cost more, the bread or the fish? _____

2. Which cost more, the bread or the tomatoes? _____

3. Order the price of each item from least to greatest.

_____

College Classes Joseph is taking a number of college classes. A course number identifies each class. Right now he is taking classes 1.31, 1.058, 2.415, 2.412, and 1.06.

4. Which of Joseph's classes has the highest course number? _____

5. Which of Joseph's classes has the lowest course number? _____

6. How many classes have course numbers that are greater than 1.50? _____

7. **Writing in Math** Is 1.5 greater than or less than 1.05? Explain.

_____

_____

_____

_____

_____

_____

Place-Value Patterns

Janine runs a business from her home. Last year she used 21,500 sheets of paper.

1. If Janine uses 10 times as much paper this year as she did last year, how much paper will she use this year?

   _____

2. A company buys paper from the same manufacturer that Janine does. If the company used 1,000 times as much paper last year as Janine did, how much paper did it use?

   _____

The area of Canada is about 10,000,000 sq km. Of that area, 9,100,000 sq km are land and 900,000 sq km are freshwater.

3. How many thousands of square kilometers of area does Canada have?

   _____

4. How many hundreds of square kilometers of Canada is freshwater?

   _____

5. **Writing in Math** Gina says that you can tell how many tens, hundreds, or thousands are in a number by moving the decimal point. Is she correct? Why or why not?

   _____

   _____

   _____

   _____

Name_____

Read and Understand

Exercise Each summer Mikael changes his workout routine by
exercising 190 min more each week. Over the summer months,
Mikael exercises a total of 910 min a week. How many minutes
a week does he work out when it is not summer?

> **Read and Understand**

Step 1: What do you know?

1. Tell the problem in your own words.

_____

2. Identify key facts and details.

_____

_____

_____

Step 2: What are you trying to find?

3. Tell what the question is asking.

_____

_____

4. Show the main idea.

5. Solve the problem. Write the answer in a complete sentence.

_____

_____

Adding and Subtracting Mentally

Aluminum Cans Jameson, Margie, Julie, and Mark collected cans for recycling to earn money for a service project. The table shows how many cans they collected during the week.

Cans Collected	
Jameson	236
Mark	171
Julio	292
Margie	300

1. How many cans did Jameson and Mark collect altogether?

_____

2. How many cans did Margie and Julie collect altogether?

_____

3. How many more cans did Julie collect than Mark?

_____

4. How many more cans did Margie collect than Jameson?

_____

5. What is the total number of cans collected by the four students?

_____

6. **Writing in Math** Describe two ways that you can add 1,820 + 230 mentally.

_____

_____

_____

_____

_____

_____

Name_____

Rounding Whole Numbers and Decimals

Continents The table shows the sizes of the three largest continents on Earth.

Earth's Continents

Continent	Area (sq km)
Asia	44,485,900
Africa	30,269,680
North America	24,235,280

1. Round the area of each continent to the nearest hundred thousand.

_____

_____

_____

2. Round the area of each continent to the nearest ten million.

_____

_____

Shopping Jeremy has $13.29 in his pocket. He buys a book for $4.99, a stuffed monkey for $3.79, and a box of pencils for $1.49.

3. Round the amount of money Jeremy has to the nearest dollar. _____

4. Round each of Jeremy's purchases to the nearest 10 cents.

_____

5. **Writing in Math** Rock says that 15.452 rounded to the nearest hundredth is 15.44, because the 2 is less than 5. Is he correct? Why or why not?

_____

_____

_____

_____

Name_____

Estimating Sums and Differences

Driving Joe is a traveling salesperson. He has started keeping track of the number of miles he drives each week on slips of paper.

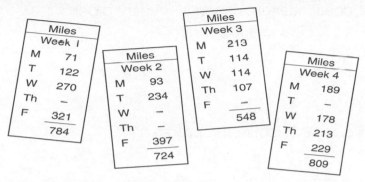

	Miles Week 1
M	71
T	122
W	270
Th	–
F	321
	784

	Miles Week 2
M	93
T	234
W	–
Th	–
F	397
	724

	Miles Week 3
M	213
T	114
W	114
Th	107
F	–
	548

	Miles Week 4
M	189
T	–
W	178
Th	213
F	229
	809

1. Joe wants to estimate how many miles he drove during Weeks 1 and 2. About how many miles did Joe drive during the first two weeks?

_____

2. About how many miles did Joe drive during Weeks 2 and 3 altogether?

_____

3. About how many more miles did Joe drive during Week 2 than Week 3? _____

4. About how many miles did Joe travel during Week 4? _____

5. About how many miles did Joe travel during all four weeks?

_____

6. Writing in Math Explain why in some instances it is better to round up, even if the numbers suggest you should not.

_____

_____

_____

Name_____

Plan and Solve

Ages Jennifer is 4 years older than her sister Jessica. Jessica is 6 years younger than her cousin Jason. Jason is 3 years older than his brother Sam, who is 13. How old is Jennifer?

> **Plan and Solve**

Step 1: Choose a strategy.

1. What strategy should you use to solve the problem?

_____

Step 2: Stuck? Don't give up. Retrace your own steps.

2. What is something you can do if you get stuck?

_____

_____

Step 3: Answer the question in the problem.

3. How old is Jennifer?

_____

4. Every day for the last three weeks Jaecinda has done as many sit-ups as she can. The first week she did 20 sit-ups, the second week she did 27 sit-ups, and the third week she did 34 sit-ups. If she continues at the same pace, how many sit-ups will she do during the fifth week?

_____

_____

_____

© Pearson Education, Inc. 5

Name_____

Adding and Subtracting Whole Numbers

Tab Collection For every tab top off an aluminum can that is turned in at an elementary school, the school receives a nickel toward buying computers. The classrooms turned in their tabs by grade. The first grade turned in 2,638 tabs, the second grade turned in 1,472 tabs, the third grade turned in 4,742 tabs, the fourth grade turned in 6,781 tabs, and the fifth grade turned in 8,979 tabs.

1. How many tabs did the first and second grades turn in altogether?

_____

2. How many more tabs did the fourth grade turn in than the third grade?

_____

Classic Cars One type of classic car was first made in 1964. The table shows the number of this type of classic car that was made each year from 1965 through 1970.

Year	Classic Cars Made
1965	559,451
1966	607,568
1967	472,121
1968	317,404
1969	310,454
1970	190,727

3. How many cars were made in 1966 and 1967 altogether?

_____

4. How many cars were made in 1968 and 1969 altogether?

_____

5. How many more cars were made in 1965 than in 1969? _____

6. **Writing in Math** Explain how you found your answer to Exercise 5.

_____

_____

_____

Adding Decimals

Fabric Lauren works at a textile mill. She weaves special fabric, which is used to make rugs. On Monday she wove 7.21 yd, on Tuesday she wove 9.653 yd, on Wednesday she wove 6.57 yd, on Thursday she wove 8.56 yd, and on Friday she wove 7.08 yd.

1. How many yards of fabric did Lauren weave from Monday through Wednesday?   _____

2. How many yards of fabric did Lauren weave during the entire week?   _____

Earnings This week Jonathan's mother gave him $1.75 for doing the laundry, $2.50 for taking care of her fish, and $1.50 for taking out the trash. He had $4.81 left from his earnings last week, and he found a quarter in the laundry.

3. How much money did Jonathan earn this week?   _____

4. How much money does Jonathan have now?   _____

5. If Jonathan earns another $3.50 doing chores at two of the neighbors' homes, how much will he have?   _____

6. **Writing in Math** Chris says that 2.05 + 1.3 is 2.18. Is he correct? Explain.

   _____

   _____

   _____

   _____

   _____

Subtracting Decimals

County Fair The largest tomato at a county fair weighed
7.29 lb. The largest pumpkin weighed 572.14 lb. The grand
champion hog weighed in at 321.09 lb.

1. How much more did the largest pumpkin
   weigh than the grand champion hog?   _____

2. How much more did the largest pumpkin
   weigh than the largest tomato?   _____

3. How much more did the grand champion
   hog weigh than the largest tomato?   _____

At the county fair, tickets for the rides can be bought in sheets of
40 for $10.00, sheets of 100 for $20.00, or each ticket for $0.50.

4. Craig came to the fair with $50.00. He
   bought a sheet of 100 tickets and bought
   dinner for $7.81. How much money does
   Craig have left?   _____

5. Tyrell came to the fair with $25.00. He
   spent $13.00 trying to win a prize, and
   then bought a necklace for $8.69. How
   much money does Tyrell have left?   _____

6. **Writing in Math** Explain why you might need to add zeros
   to the end of a decimal in order to subtract.

_____

_____

_____

_____

_____

Name_____

Look Back and Check

Cargo Ship A cargo ship arrives empty in California and loads 42,692 crates. It leaves California and travels to a port in Alaska, where it unloads 27,450 crates. It then goes to a second Alaskan port and unloads another 12,728 crates. When it arrives at the third port, it unloads the rest of the crates. How many crates were unloaded at the third port?

Melissa solved the problem as shown below.

```
   3 12
   4̶2,692      crates loaded
 - 27,450      crates unloaded at 1st stop
   15,242      crates left after 1st stop

     4 123 12
   1̶5̶,2̶4̶2̶      crates left after 1st stop
 - 12,728      crates unloaded at 2nd stop
    2,524      crates left after 2nd stop
```

Step 1: Have you checked your answer?

1. Was the correct question answered? Explain.

_____

_____

_____

Step 2: Have you checked your work?

2. Was Melissa's final answer correct? Explain.

_____

_____

_____

_____

PROBLEM-SOLVING APPLICATIONS

Trombone

Garrett is renting a trombone for $50.00 a month. He can buy a used trombone for $200.00 from a student who played last year. How long will it take Garrett to spend as much in rental fees as it would cost to buy the used trombone?

Read and Understand

1. How much does it cost to rent a trombone for one month?   _____

2. How much does it cost to buy a used trombone?   _____

Plan and Solve

3. What strategy will you use?   _____

4. Solve the problem. Write your answer in a complete sentence.

_____

_____

Look Back and Check

5. Explain how you can check your answer.

_____

Solve Another Problem

6. At the beginning of one week, a large paper company purchased 120,000 boxes of paper. The same week the company sold 92,000 boxes of paper. There were 46,000 boxes of paper left at the end of the week. How many boxes of paper did the company begin the week with?

_____

Multiplication Patterns

New Bats As a gift, a baseball league will receive new bats for each of its teams. Each team will receive 4 new bats.

1. The league now has 8 teams with 5 bats each. What is the total number of bats the league has before the addition of the new bats?   _____

2. What will the total number of bats be after the addition of the new bats?   _____

The table at the right shows the average number of cans Daniel collected each day during June, July, and August.

Month	Cans per Day
June (30 days)	11
July (31 days)	10
August (31 days)	15

3. How many cans did Daniel collect for the month of June?

_____

4. How many cans did Daniel collect for the month of July?   _____

5. How many cans did Daniel collect for the month of August?   _____

6. **Writing in Math** Daniel received $2 for every 100 cans he turned in to the recycling center. Explain how you could determine mentally about how much money Daniel made collecting cans for each of the three months.

_____

_____

_____

_____

Estimating Products

Backpacking A backpacking club is planning a 12-day trip.
There are 14 members in the club.

1. Each member of the club eats 2 lb of food each day. Write
   and solve an expression you could use to overestimate
   how much food the club should bring.

   _____

2. Overestimate how many pounds of food would be needed
   if 4 of the members brought along 1 friend each.

   _____

3. Estimate the cost of 4 winter coats
   in 1930.

   _____

Item	Cost in 1930
Winter coat	$28
Sewing machine	$24
Gas stove	$21

4. Estimate the cost today of buying
   8 sewing machines if each machine
   costs $285. Estimate the cost today for
   9 gas stoves if each stove costs $582.

   _____

   _____

5. **Writing in Math** Explain how you estimated the costs in
   Exercise 4. Was your answer an overestimate or an
   underestimate?

   _____

   _____

   _____

Mental Math: Using the Distributive Property

Allan drives every day for his business.

Day	Miles
Monday	72
Tuesday	84
Wednesday	84
Thursday	72
Friday	84

1. Use the Distributive Property to mentally determine how many miles Allan drove on Monday and Thursday combined.

   _____

2. Use the Distributive Property to mentally determine how many miles Allan drove on Tuesday, Wednesday, and Friday combined.

   _____

Measurements Use what you know about the Distributive Property and the table to mentally answer Exercises 3–5.

Area Conversions

1 sq ft = 144 sq in.
1 sq yd = 9 sq ft
1 sq mi = 640 acres

3. How many square feet are there in 72 sq yd?

   _____

4. How many acres are there in 21 sq mi?

   _____

5. **Writing in Math** Explain how you used the Distributive Property to solve Exercise 4.

   _____

   _____

   _____

   _____

Multiplying Whole Numbers

Earth Years The table shows the length of a year (in Earth years) for each of the outer planets of our solar system: Jupiter, Saturn, Uranus, Neptune, and Pluto. One Earth year is approximately 365 days, 52 weeks, or 12 months long.

Planet	Length of Year (in Earth years)
Jupiter	12
Saturn	29
Uranus	84
Neptune	165
Pluto	249

1. How many days long is a year on Jupiter?

   _____

2. How many weeks long is a year on Saturn?

   _____

3. How many months long is a year on Pluto? _____

Savings Account Calvin's mother started a savings account for him when he was born. Every month his mother deposited $25 into his account. She continued depositing $25 every month until he was 18 years old.

4. How much money did Calvin's mother deposit into his account each year?

   _____

5. How much money had Calvin's mother deposited into his savings account by the end of his 18th year?

   _____

6. **Writing in Math** Explain how you solved Exercise 5.

   _____

   _____

   _____

Name_____

Choose a Computation Method

Appliances The amount of energy used by different appliances is expressed in kilowatt-hours. The estimated annual kilowatt-hours per household for several different appliances are shown.

Appliance	Kilowatt-hours per Year
Blender	15
Toaster	39
Color television	502

1. How many kilowatt-hours would a blender use over 8 years? Tell what computation method you used.

_____

2. How many kilowatt-hours would a toaster use over 8 years? Tell what computation method you used.

_____

3. How many kilowatt-hours would a color television use over 11 years? Tell what computation method you used.

_____

Customers at a berry stand can purchase berries that have already been picked, or they can pick the berries themselves. Already-picked strawberries are $3 per basket. U-pick strawberries are $2 per basket. Already-picked blueberries are $5 per basket. U-pick blueberries are $4 per basket.

4. How much would 5 baskets of already-picked strawberries, 5 baskets of already-picked blueberries, 4 baskets of U-pick strawberries, and 3 baskets of U-pick blueberries cost? _____

5. **Writing in Math** For Exercise 4, did you use mental math, paper and pencil, or a calculator to determine the answer? Explain your choice.

_____

_____

_____

PROBLEM-SOLVING STRATEGY   PS 2-6

Make an Organized List

Alex and Yvonne are spending the day at
Family Fun Park. They have $50 to spend
between them. How many combinations
of activities can Alex and Yvonne do for
under $50?

Family Fun Park

Activity	Price
Water slides	$9
Miniature golf	$5
Mountain bikes	$15

Read and Understand

1. How much will each activity cost for both of them?

_____

Plan and Solve

2. What strategy will you use?

_____

3. Which combinations will work?

_____

_____

4. Write the answer in a complete sentence.

_____

_____

Look Back and Check

5. Explain how you can check if your work is correct.

_____

_____

Decimal Patterns

Speed of Light Light travels at a speed of 300,000 km per second. Because objects are so far apart in space, scientists use the light-year to measure the distances between objects in space. A light-year is the distance light travels in one year. The table below shows the number of light-years between three stars and the Sun.

Star	Distance from Sun (in light-years)
Barnard's Star	5.94
Wolf 359	7.80
Sirius A, B	8.60

1. If a star were 10 times farther away from the Sun than Barnard's Star, how far away would it be?

   _____

2. If a star were 100 times farther away from the Sun than Wolf 359, how far away would it be?

   _____

3. If a star were 1,000 times farther away from the Sun than Sirius A, B, how far away would it be?

   _____

4. **Writing in Math** Explain the difference between multiplying a decimal by 10 and multiplying the same decimal by 1,000.

   _____

   _____

   _____

   _____

Estimating Decimal Products

Brenton is making pancakes for his family's breakfast. His measuring spoons and cups are all metric so he must convert the quantities in the recipe. The table below shows the conversions.

1 tsp	= 4.93 mL
1 tbsp	= 14.77 mL
1 c	= 236.64 mL

1. Brenton must use 2.25 tsp of baking soda and 3 tbsp of melted butter in his pancakes. Estimate to determine about how many milliliters 2.25 tsp and 3 tbsp will be.

_____

2. The recipe calls for 2.25 c of flour. Estimate to determine about how many milliliters 2.25 c will be.

_____

Marcie is making a new dress for herself. She buys 3.5 yd of white fabric at $4.80 per yard and 2.5 yd of blue fabric at $3.35 per yard.

3. Find an overestimate and an underestimate for the price of the white fabric.

_____

4. Find an overestimate and an underestimate for the price of the blue fabric.

_____

5. **Writing in Math** Explain how an overestimate and an underestimate can be used to find a reasonable estimate.

_____

_____

Multiplying Whole Numbers and Decimals

Life Spans Animals age at different rates. The average life span of several animals is shown.

Average Life Spans

Domestic dog	12 years
Kangaroo	7 years
Rabbit	5 years

1. What is the average life span of black bears if it is 3.6 times greater than the life span of rabbits? _____

2. What is the average life span of Asian elephants if it is 5.7 times greater than the life span of kangaroos? _____

Supply Shopping Kisha is going shopping for back-to-school supplies. She needs 4 three-ring notebooks, 6 folders, 3 highlighting pens in different colors, and 2 pencil boxes.

3. How much will the notebooks cost if they are $3.49 each? _____

4. How much will the folders cost if they are $1.17 each? _____

5. Which will cost more, the highlighting pens at $1.23 each or the pencil boxes at $1.32 each?

_____

6. **Writing in Math** Explain how you know that the product of 8×0.9 is less than 8.

_____

_____

_____

Using Grids to Multiply Decimals by Decimals

Water Containers Justin has two containers, one that holds 0.8 gal of water and one that holds 0.6 gal of water. He brought the containers to a soccer game he was playing in.

1. One of Justin's teammates drank 4 tenths of the larger container of water. How many gallons did he drink?

   _____

2. Justin drank 7 tenths of the smaller container of water. How much water did Justin drink?

   _____

Knotted Rope A rope has knots tied at specific intervals along its length. The total length of the rope is 0.9 yd.

3. The first knot is at a spot that is 0.2 of the total length of the rope. Where is the first knot?

   _____

4. A second knot is located 0.2 of the way past the first knot. Where is the second knot?

   _____

5. Where is the halfway point on the rope?

   _____

6. **Writing in Math** Tell what the grids and the shaded areas represent.

   _____

   _____

   _____

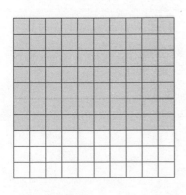 × 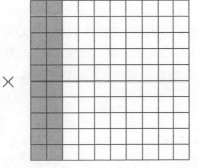 =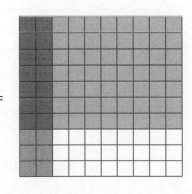

Multiplying Decimals by Decimals

Surface Area The table below shows the surface area of several items. The area is expressed in square inches.

Item	Surface Area (in square inches)
Sheet of paper ($8\frac{1}{2}$ in. by 11 in.)	93.5
Playing card	7.6
Postage stamps	0.85

1. What is the surface area of 2.5 sheets of paper? _____

2. If postage stamps were 1.25 times larger than they are now, what would their surface area be? _____

3. If postage stamps were 1.75 times larger than they are now, what would their surface area be? _____

Fruit Connie's mother sends her to the store to buy nectarines and cherries. The nectarines are $1.50 per pound and the cherries are $2.60 per pound.

4. Connie buys 4.5 lb of nectarines. How much did she pay? _____

5. Connie really likes cherries and wants to buy 2.5 lb with her own money. She has $5.00 of her own money in her pocket. Can she buy that many pounds of cherries?

_____

6. **Writing in Math** Elizabeth says that if you multiply a decimal with 2 decimal places by a decimal with 3 decimal places, the product will have 6 decimal places because $2 \times 3 = 6$. Is she correct? Explain.

_____

_____

Variables and Expressions

Shopping Spree Moira is spending the day clothes shopping with her sister, Brianne. The girls plan on using several discount coupons on their shopping spree.

1. Brianne buys a pullover that, when combined with her coupon for $x off, brings the total cost down to $38. Write an algebraic expression to represent the original cost of the pullover.   _____

2. Moira buys a pair of pants that have a price tag of $p. She uses a $3-off coupon to reduce the price. Write an algebraic expression to represent the reduced price of the pants.   _____

Phone Plan Rick's new long distance phone plan allows him to call anywhere in the country for $0.05 per minute on weekends and evenings and $0.07 per minute on weekdays. Martin's long distance phone plan allows him to call anywhere in the country at any time for $0.08 per minute.

3. Write an expression that represents the cost of an r-minute weekend phone call for Rick and an r-minute weekend phone call for Martin.

_____

_____

4. If a weekday phone call for Martin is represented by $0.08 \times n$, evaluate for $n = 35$, 45, and 55 min.

_____

_____

5. **Writing in Math** Explain how you would find the length of a $5.00 long-distance phone call that costs $0.10 per minute.

_____

_____

Name_____

Translating Words into Expressions

Bookstore A bookstore is reorganizing its books. All of the books are being removed from their shelves and put in different locations. There are y identical bookcases in the store. Each bookcase holds 78 books.

1. Which expression shows the total number of books that can be stacked on all the bookcases, $y + 78$, $78 \div y$, or $78y$? _____

2. Each bookcase has z individual shelves. Which expression shows how many books can be put on each shelf, $78 + z$, $78 \div z$, or $78z$? _____

Plant Food Ashanti is giving her houseplants several different kinds of plant food. She reads the labels carefully to make sure she does not give too much or too little to her plants.

3. The label on plant food A says to add one part food supplement to every two parts water. Write an algebraic expression that represents the amount of plant food A that is to be added to an amount w of water. _____

4. The label on plant food B says to add 1.25 tsp of food supplement to every cup of water. Write an algebraic expression that represents the amount of plant food B that is to be added to c cups of water. _____

5. Plant food C is sprinkled around the base of the plant once every d days. Write an algebraic expression that represents the number of times per year plant food C is used. _____

6. **Writing in Math** Write what the expression $(2 \times 87) - l$ means.

_____

_____

Name_____

Find a Rule

Typing Class Eric took a typing class in school. By the end of the class, he was able to type 65 words per minute with errors and 55 words per minute without errors.

1. Complete the table to show how many words, with errors, Eric types in 1, 2, 3, 4, and 5 min.

Minutes	Words

2. Complete the table to show how many words, without errors, Eric types in 1, 2, 3, 4, and 5 min.

Minutes	Words

3. What is the rule for the table you made in Exercise 1?

_____

4. What is the rule for the table you made in Exercise 2?

_____

5. **Writing in Math** Explain the relationship between a rule and an input/output table.

_____

Solving Equations

Eggs for Sale The Egg-Rite Hatchery sells fresh eggs. Eggs are collected each morning, packed into egg cartons, and then sold. Each carton holds 12 eggs.

1. One day the hatchery sold 20 cartons of eggs. Write and solve an equation that shows how many eggs were sold. Let e equal the number of eggs sold.

   _____

2. On another day the hatchery sold 276 eggs. Write and solve an equation that shows how many cartons were sold. Let c equal the number of cartons.

   _____

Savings Audrey has been saving $20 a month from her allowance for 5 years. She plans to use the money to buy a new computer.

3. There are 12 months in one year. Solve the equation $5 \times 12 = w$ to find the number of months in 5 years.

   _____

4. Using your answer from Exercise 3, write and solve an equation to find how much money Audrey has saved in 5 years. Let m be the amount of money.

   _____

   _____

5. **Writing in Math** Explain how a variable is used in an equation.

   _____

   _____

   _____

© Pearson Education, Inc. 5

PROBLEM-SOLVING APPLICATIONS

Photo Collection

Amy has three photos that she wants to display on a shelf in her bedroom, with the photos lined up in a row. One photo is of her brother, another is of her sister, and the third is of her parents. In how many ways can she arrange the photos?

Read and Understand

1. What do you know?

_____

_____

2. What are you trying to find?

_____

_____

Plan and Solve

3. What strategy will you use?

_____

4. Write the answer in a complete sentence.

_____

_____

Look Back and Check

5. Is your work correct? Explain.

_____

_____

_____

The Meaning of Division

1. Cara plans to spend 1 day per week working on her social studies paper, which is due in 4 weeks. If the social studies paper is 8 pages long, how many pages will she write per day until she is finished?

_____

2. Cara's short story is due in 3 weeks. She plans to spend 4 days per week working on the paper. If the short story is 25 pages long, how many pages will she write per day until she is finished? Will Cara's plan work?

_____

_____

_____

Salad Dressing Bryan is making salad and two kinds of salad dressing for the weekend picnic. He has decided to make an Italian dressing and a lemon herb dressing.

3. To make 4 batches of Italian dressing, Bryan uses 36 tsp of olive oil. There are 3 tsp in a tablespoon. If Bryan had used a tablespoon to measure the olive oil, how many would he have used to make 4 batches?   _____

4. To make 2 batches of the lemon herb dressing, Bryan uses 8 c of vinegar. If there are 4 c in 1 qt, how many quarts of vinegar will Bryan use to make the lemon herb dressing?   _____

5. **Writing in Math** Explain how Exercise 4 could be made into a multiplication problem.

_____

_____

Division Patterns

Quarter Chain The Park Valley High School students tried to build the longest continuous chain of quarters. The two-day fundraiser raised more than $1,000 for the school.

1. By the end of the two-day fundraiser, there were 6,000 quarters in the chain. If 1 quarter is about 1 inch in diameter, about how many feet long was the chain? (Remember: There are 12 inches in 1 foot.) _____

2. How many dollars did the Park Valley High School quarter chain represent? _____

Savings Bond Jack and Martha have decided to cash out a savings bond they received for their marriage 25 years ago. The current value of the bond is $50,000.

3. If Jack and Martha decide to have the value of the bond paid to them in $100 bills, how many bills will they receive? _____

4. How many $20 bills would Jack and Martha receive from the $50,000? _____

5. How many $50 bills would Jack and Martha receive? _____

6. **Writing in Math** Explain the pattern that helps you solve $40 \div 8$ and $40,000 \div 8$.

_____

_____

_____

_____

_____

_____

Name_____

Estimating Quotients

Type of Elephant	Weight (kg)
African (male)	5,400–7,200
Indian (male)	3,200

1. Estimate how many tons an African elephant weighs if 889.96 kg equal 1 T.

   _____

2. Using the same information, find about how many tons the Indian elephant weighs.

   _____

Food for Wildlife The Rock Creek Wildlife Preserve records the amount of food that is used. The table shows the amount of food used during a 6-month period.

Wildlife Food Used—Jan. to June

Type of Food	Amount
Millet	289 lb
Sunflower seeds	332 lb
Peanuts	622 lb

3. About how many pounds of sunflower seeds did the preserve use per month?

   _____

4. About how many pounds combined of millet and sunflower seeds did the preserve use in 2 months?

   _____

5. About how many pounds of peanuts did the preserve use in 3 months?

   _____

6. **Writing in Math** Explain why it is easier to estimate quotients when dividing large numbers.

   _____

   _____

   _____

Name_____

Look for a Pattern

Study the picture for number patterns. Then write the missing numbers to complete the pattern.

┌─────────────────────────────┐
│ **Read and Understand**   │
└─────────────────────────────┘

1. What are you trying to find?

_____

_____

┌─────────────────────────────┐
│ **Plan and Solve**   │
└─────────────────────────────┘

2. For every number in the picture, name the two numbers that are directly above it.

_____

3. What relationship does each pair of numbers have to the number below it?

_____

_____

4. Write the missing numbers that complete the pattern.   _____

┌─────────────────────────────┐
│ **Look Back and Check**   │
└─────────────────────────────┘

5. Explain how you can check your answer.

_____

_____

Name_____

Understanding Division

Ashanti and four of her friends have set up a refreshment stand in their neighborhood. The list shows the prices for a cup of each item sold at the stand.

Refreshment Stand
Lemonade—$0.50 per cup
Strawberries—$1.00 per cup
Blackberries—$1.50 per cup

1. The first weekend, the stand made $26 selling lemonade, $37 selling strawberries, and $42 selling blackberries. How many cups of each item were sold during the first week? What was the total dollar amount sold?

_____

_____

_____

2. If the total sales are divided equally, how much money will each person get? _____

Vacation Spending Jonah is on a 5-day vacation with his parents in San Diego, California. He has been given $150 to spend on souvenirs and $200 to spend on meals and snacks.

3. Jonah would like to spend his souvenir money equally from day to day. How much money will Jonah spend on souvenirs each day? _____

4. If Jonah does the same with his meal and snack money, how much money will he spend each day? _____

5. **Writing in Math** Explain how the steps in division can be used to show how money is shared.

_____

_____

_____

Dividing Whole Numbers

1. A hamster's heart beats 280 times per minute, and a gray whale's heart beats 8 times per minute. How many times faster does a hamster's heart beat than a gray whale's?

_____

2. A sea otter can hold its breath under water for 5 min, and a bottlenose whale can hold its breath for 120 min. How many times greater is the time a bottlenose whale can hold its breath than the time a sea otter can hold its breath?

_____

Calories Different amounts of calories are burned, or used, by the human body during different activities. The table shows the number of calories burned per minute during different activities by a person who weighs 125 lb.

Calories Burned per Minute

Activity	Calories Burned
Skateboarding	5
Waterskiing	6
Tai chi	4

3. Gizelle burned 615 calories skateboarding. How many minutes did she spend skateboarding?

_____

4. Carlos spent 140 min waterskiing on Sunday and 70 min practicing tai chi on Monday. How many times more calories did he burn waterskiing?

_____

5. **Writing in Math** Explain how you can tell when division must be used to solve a number problem.

_____

_____

_____

_____

Name_____

Zeros in the Quotient

1. If it takes Martin 3 hr to travel from Pittsburgh to Memphis, how many miles per hour will he be traveling?

Air Distance from Pittsburgh

Destination City	Miles (One Way)
Memphis	660
Omaha	836

_____

2. Martin's trip from Pittsburgh to Omaha takes 4 hr. How many miles per hour will he be traveling on this trip?

_____

Object or Event	Length, Height, or Distance
Longest home run	618 ft
Length of QE2 ocean liner	963 ft
Height of Saturn rocket	364 ft

3. How many yards is the longest home run? (Hint: There are 3 ft in 1 yd.)   _____

4. The length of a table-tennis table is 9 ft. How many table-tennis tables can fit end-to-end along the length of the QE2 ocean liner?

_____

5. About how many table-tennis tables can fit end-to-end along the distance covered by the Saturn rocket?

_____

6. **Writing in Math** Explain what the zero represents in the quotient for 648 ÷ 6.

_____

_____

Name_____

Dividing Larger Dividends

Ms. Fischer's science classes are working on experiments to examine the growth rate of sunflower seedlings in different types of soil.

1. Over the course of 6 days, Ms. Fischer's classes used a total of 1,984 lb of potting soil for their experiments. If 8 teams worked on the project, how many pounds of soil did each team use? _____

2. A total of 2,464 sunflower seeds were used for the experiments. How many seeds did each of the 8 teams use? _____

The three highest mountain peaks in the world are Mt. Everest, K2, and Mt. Kangchenjunga in the Himalayas. The heights of these peaks are shown in the table.

Mountain	Height	
Everest	29,035 ft	8,850 m
K2	28,250 ft	8,611 m
Kangchenjunga	28,169 ft	8,586 m

3. A climbing team begins their final climb to the peak of Mt. Everest at about 5,000 m. How many meters will they climb each day if it takes them 5 days to complete their climb?

_____

4. A team climbing Kangchenjunga begins their final climb at 21,750 ft. How many feet will they average per day if it takes them 4 days to complete the climb?

_____

5. **Writing in Math** Explain why a zero is not placed in front of the eight in the quotient for 640 ÷ 8.

_____

_____

Name_____

Dividing Money

Shopping Monica went back-to-school clothes shopping and bought 4 sweaters for a total of $185.00. She also spent a total of $119.85 on 3 pairs of corduroy pants.

1. How much did each sweater cost?   _____

2. How much did each pair of pants cost?   _____

Dining Out Some teachers at River Valley High School went out to dinner to celebrate the beginning of the school year. The bill for the 9 faculty members came to $167.40.

3. The group decided to split the dinner bill
   equally. How much did each person pay?   _____

4. The group decided to leave a tip of $33.75.
   How much did each person pay if the tip
   was divided equally?   _____

5. After dinner, the group went to a different
   restaurant for dessert. The total bill was
   $80.55. If the group decided to split this
   bill equally, how much did each person pay? _____

6. **Writing in Math** Explain how you know where the decimal
   point goes in the quotient when an amount of money is
   being divided by a whole number.

   _____

   _____

   _____

   _____

   _____

   _____

   _____

Name_____

Factors and Divisibility

Jordan is trying to figure out how to arrange the plants in her vegetable garden. She is planting cabbage and string bean seedlings.

1. Jordan has 24 string bean seedlings. How many different planting arrangements are possible for the string beans?

   _____

2. There are 28 cabbage plants. How many different planting arrangements are possible for the cabbages?

   _____

Mr. Baldwin is planning the testing schedule for his classes. For the month of April, he would like to space his tests out evenly. (Remember: There are 30 days in April.)

3. Mr. Baldwin plans to give 5 science tests. How many days apart will each science test be?   _____

4. There are 2 social studies tests to be given during the month. How many days apart will these tests be given?   _____

5. If Mr. Baldwin gives 3 math tests, how many days apart will they be given?   _____

6. **Writing in Math** Explain why the answers for Exercises 3–5 would be different for the month of March. (Hint: How many days are in March?)

   _____

   _____

   _____

   _____

Prime and Composite Numbers

River Lengths The approximate length of four major rivers is given in the table to the right.

River	Approximate Length (miles)
Missouri	2,315
Yukon	1,979
Tocantins	1,677
Don	1,223

1. For which of the rivers would it be possible for towns to be located at equal distances along the river's length?

   _____

   _____

2. For which of the rivers would it not be possible for towns to be located at equal distances along the river's length? Explain.

   _____

   _____

   _____

3. By what distance would towns be separated if they were located at equal lengths along the Missouri River or the Tocantins River?

   _____

   _____

4. **Writing in Math** Explain how you found which river lengths were prime and which were not.

   _____

   _____

   _____

   _____

Name_____

Interpreting Remainders

Olympic Mountain Hike Ten hikers set out on a route that covers 51 mi through the Olympic Mountains of Washington. Each hiker is carrying a 30 lb backpack. If they hike 4 mi per day, how many days will it take the hikers to complete the route?

> **Read and Understand**

1. What is the total mileage of the route?   _____

2. How many miles will the hikers travel per day? _____

3. What are you trying to find?

_____

_____

> **Plan and Solve**

4. Write and solve a number sentence.

_____

5. Write the answer in a complete sentence.

_____

_____

> **Look Back and Check**

6. Explain what the remainder of 3 represents.

_____

_____

_____

Name_____

Order of Operations

Emilio and Steven are buying flowers for their mothers. The table shows the price of each type of flower.

Amaryllis—$4 each
Baby's breath—$1 bunch
Carnation—$2 for 2
Rose—$3 each
Sunflower—$3 each

1. Emilio selects 2 amaryllis flowers, 2 carnations, and 2 bunches of baby's breath for his bouquet. Write an expression with parentheses to represent the cost of Emilio's bouquet.

_____

2. Steven selects 1 sunflower, 1 carnation, and 2 roses for his bouquet. The sunflower is discounted $1 because it is slightly smaller than the other sunflowers. Write an expression with parentheses to represent the cost of Steven's bouquet.

_____

Mrs. Campbell is organizing the textbooks in her classroom. She starts by stacking all of the textbooks according to subject.

3. After stacking, Mrs. Campbell has 4 stacks of 10 science books, 3 stacks of 8 history books, and 6 stacks of 5 mathematics books. Write an expression to represent the total number of books.

_____

4. Mr. Barber, another teacher, takes 3 science books. Write an expression to represent the total number of Mrs. Campbell's science books and the books taken by Mr. Barber. _____

5. **Writing in Math** Explain how the expression in Exercise 4 would be different if no parentheses were used.

_____

_____

Name_____

Graphing Ordered Pairs

Rachel's Room Rachel's bedroom is shown on the grid. The positions of the windows, the door, the closet, and her bed are represented by ordered pairs.

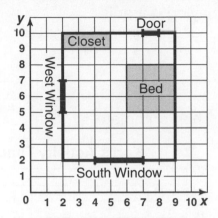

1. What pairs of coordinates describe the position of each of the two windows on the grid?

_____

_____

2. What pairs of coordinates describe the four corners of Rachel's bed?

_____

3. Rachel would like to put a nightstand next to her bed on the side closest to the south window. What four pairs of coordinates show where the nightstand should be placed?

_____

4. **Writing in Math** Explain how coordinates on a grid can describe a line that is twice as long as another line.

_____

_____

_____

Name_____

Rules, Tables, and Graphs

Playing Guitar Karl's favorite activity is playing guitar. He plays guitar every day for 3 times the amount of time he spends reading.

1. Write a rule to show that the time spent playing guitar is 3 times the time spent reading.

_____

2. Complete the table of values for the rule. Then complete the graph for your table of values.

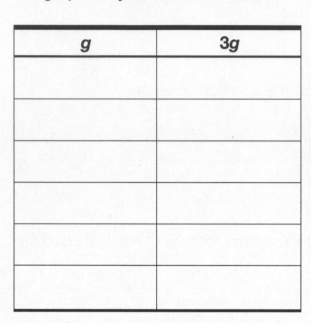

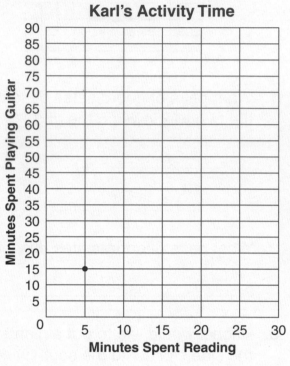

3. **Writing in Math** Explain why it is easier to understand information presented in a table by graphing it.

_____

_____

_____

_____

Name_____

Planting Trees

The Longbow Forestry Service is replacing trees that were
harvested during a recent deforestation project. They have
762 fir trees and 751 spruce trees to replant on 6 hillsides.
The service would like to plant equal numbers of trees on
each hillside. How many fir trees and how many spruce trees
will the forestry service plant on each hillside?

Read and Understand

1. What are you trying to find?

_____

_____

Plan and Solve

2. Write and solve a number sentence for the number of each
   kind of tree to be replanted.

_____

_____

3. Write the answer in a complete sentence.

_____

_____

_____

Look Back and Check

4. Explain how you can check your answer.

_____

_____

Dividing by Multiples of 10

Library Books The school library is filled with specially made book cabinets. Each cabinet has 10 shelves. Each shelf can hold 40 books.

1. How many shelves are needed to fit 1,440 books? _____

2. How many cabinets are needed to fit 2,400 books? _____

3. The students have checked out 360 books. How many shelves are needed when the books are returned? _____

Bakery A bakery made muffins that were sold to both grocery stores and restaurants. The muffins that were sold to the grocery store were packed 50 muffins to a box. The muffins that were sold to restaurants were packed 20 muffins to a box.

4. If 4,000 muffins were sold to a grocery store, how many boxes would there be? _____

5. If 1,000 muffins were sold to a restaurant, how many boxes would there be? _____

6. On a day the bakery made 3,000 muffins, 50 grocery store-sized boxes were packed. The remaining muffins were packed in restaurant-sized boxes. How many restaurant-sized boxes were packed?

_____

7. **Writing in Math** How many minutes equal 54,000 seconds? Explain how you used mental math to solve this problem.

_____

_____

_____

_____

_____

Estimating with Two-Digit Divisors

A public library held a used book sale. At the sale the books were placed onto tables according to the type of book. For Exercises 1–2, round to the nearest ten to estimate. The library sold 359 children's books and 912 magazines.

1. About how many children's books were placed on each of 13 tables?

_____

2. About how many magazines were placed on each of 16 tables?

_____

Planets The length of a day is different on each planet. It is determined by the speed at which the planet rotates on its axis. The length of a day on each planet, measured in Earth hours, is shown on the chart.

Planet	Length of Day (measured in Earth hours)
Mercury	1,408
Venus	5,833
Earth	24
Mars	25
Jupiter	10
Saturn	11
Uranus	17
Neptune	16
Pluto	153

3. The length of a day on Pluto is about how many times the length of a day on Saturn?

_____

4. The length of a day on Venus is about how many times the length of a day on Uranus?

_____

5. **Writing in Math** What compatible numbers would you use to compare the length of a day on Mercury to the length of a day on Neptune? Explain.

_____

_____

Name_____

Try, Check, and Revise

Library Volunteers Student volunteers reshelve books in the library at the end of each school day. On Tuesday, Allen and Bonnie both reshelved the same number of books. Kara reshelved 20 more books than Bonnie did. Together, the three volunteers reshelved 260 books. How many books did each volunteer place on the shelves?

Read and Understand

1. What is the total number of books the students reshelved? _____

2. How many students volunteered at the library? _____

Plan and Solve

3. What is a reasonable first try for solving the problem?

_____

_____

4. Does the answer fit the information given in the problem?

_____

5. Revise your first answer to make a reasonable second try.

_____

_____

6. Does your answer now fit with the information in the problem? _____

Look Back and Check

7. What other strategy could be used to solve this problem?

_____

Dividing Whole Numbers by Two-Digit Divisors

A small roadside stand sold apple juice in 64 oz cartons.

1. On Thursday, 515 oz of apple juice were produced. How many 64 oz cartons were filled? How many ounces were left over?

_____

2. On Friday, the same amount of apple juice was produced as on Thursday, but the farmer sold it in 16 oz cartons. How many 16 oz cartons were filled? How many ounces were left over?

_____

A shipment of school supplies has arrived at Rosedale School. The supplies are to be shared equally among the school's 18 classrooms.

School Supply List
Pencils – 141 boxes
Pens – 89 boxes
Notebooks – 126 boxes
Folders – 60 boxes

4. Can any of the items in the shipment be shared equally among the classrooms with none left over? If so, which items and how many for each classroom?

_____

5. How many boxes of pens can be distributed to each classroom? Are there any left over? If so, how many?

_____

6. **Writing in Math** How many boxes of folders would each of the 18 classrooms receive? What is your suggestion for the most even distribution of the remaining boxes? Explain.

_____

_____

Dividing Larger Numbers

Vacation Steve's family is thinking of taking a vacation. They have not decided where they will go, but they do know they will drive to their destination. Steve lives in Buffalo, New York. The distance to some of the possible vacation destinations is listed below.

Driving Distance

From Buffalo, New York to:	
Indianapolis	510 mi
Miami	1,445 mi
Detroit	252 mi
Seattle	2,596 mi
Washington, D.C.	386 mi

1. Steve's mom and dad plan to drive an average speed of 60 mi per hour on the trip. At that rate, which cities on the list could be reached in 20 hr of driving, or less?

   _____

2. At the same driving rate, which cities on the list could be reached in more than 20 hr, but less than 30 hr of driving?

   _____

3. **Writing in Math** Is there any city on the list that would require more than 30 hr of driving at 60 mi per hour? At that rate, how many hours of driving would it take? Explain how you know that the quotient (number of hours) would begin in the tens column.

   _____

   _____

   _____

   _____

© Pearson Education, Inc. 5

Name_____

Dividing: Choose a Computation Method

Largest Lakes Information about the 8 largest lakes in the world is listed in the chart.

Lake	Area (Square Miles)
Caspian Sea	152,239
Superior	31,820
Victoria	26,828
Huron	23,010
Michigan	22,400
Aral	13,000
Tanganyika	12,700
Baikal	12,162

1. The Caspian Sea is about how many times larger than Lake Superior?

   _____

2. Which lake is about twice as large as Lake Aral?

   _____

3. Which lake is closest to 12.5 times smaller than the Caspian Sea?

   _____

4. Which lake is about 7 times larger than Lake Michigan?

   _____

5. **Writing in Math** Explain what calculation method you would use to find 240 ÷ 60.

   _____

   _____

   _____

Dividing with Zeros in the Quotient PS 4-7

Pet Food We R Pets, a large pet store, orders dog and cat food in large shipments. Then the store bags and sells the pet food to its customers.

1. A shipment of 6,150 lb of dog food was divided into 30 lb bags. How many 30 lb bags were filled? _____

2. A shipment of 1,962 lb of cat food was divided into 18 lb bags. How many 18 lb bags could be filled? _____

3. A shipment of 4,320 lb of dog food was divided into 16 lb bags. How many 16 lb bags could be filled? _____

Recycling When the Northridge recycling center opened, many families brought their items for recycling.

4. The paper-recycling bin can hold 45 lb of paper. Every time 45 lb of paper were placed in the bin, it had to be emptied. If 4,770 lb of paper were recycled in the first week, how many times was the paper bin emptied? _____

5. The glass-recycling bin can hold 250 lb of glass. Every time 250 lb of glass were placed in the bin, it had to be emptied. If 27,450 lb of glass were recycled at Northridge, how many times was the glass bin emptied? How many more pounds need to be added before it is emptied again?

_____

6. **Writing in Math** The plastics-recycling bin can hold 55 lb of plastic. Every time 55 lb of plastic were placed in the bin, it had to be emptied. If 11,275 lb of plastic were recycled in the first week, how many times was the plastics bin emptied? Explain how you found out there was a zero in the quotient.

_____

_____

_____

Name_____

Multiple-Step Problems

In a typical 7-day week, the Staten Island Ferry takes 648 trips. There are 64 trips each weekend day. The remaining trips are equally divided between the weekdays. How many trips does the Staten Island Ferry make each weekday?

Read and Understand

1. What are you trying to find?

_____

_____

Plan and Solve

2. What is one of the hidden questions?

_____

_____

3. What is the answer to the hidden question?

_____

4. Write the answer to the problem in a complete sentence.

_____

Look Back and Check

5. Explain why your answer is logical.

_____

_____

_____

Dividing Decimals by 10, 100, and 1,000

Swim Races The Jefferson High School swim team posted its records on a sign in the gymnasium.

Swim Team Records

50 yd freestyle — 20.17 sec
100 yd freestyle — 47.83 sec
100 yd butterfly — 53.49 sec

1. What was the speed per yard of the swimmer with the butterfly-stroke record?

   _____

2. What was the speed per yard of the swimmer with the 100 yd freestyle record?

   _____

3. If the 50 yd freestyle record-holder could swim the 100 yd race in exactly double his 50 yd time, what would his speed per yard be?

   _____

Spring Fundraiser Ten students formed the school fundraising committee. The committee planned several events for the spring.

4. One of the events, the spring relay race, raised $2,190.80. How much was raised per committee member?

   _____

5. For another event, the committee members worked on a bake sale. The bake sale raised $345.60. How much was raised per worker?

   _____

6. **Writing in Math** For the spring formal fundraiser, the committee was increased to 50 members. Each member worked 2 hr. The event raised $1,267.00. How much money was raised per hour of work? Explain how and why you moved the decimal point.

   _____

   _____

   _____

Dividing Money by Two-Digit Divisors

Buying Gas The price of a gallon of gas often changes. Hector kept a record of how much gas he bought and the total cost.

1. On March 5, Hector bought 18 gal of gas for $23.22. What was the cost of each gallon of gas? _____

2. On March 12, Hector bought 20 gal of gas for $25.00. Was the cost per gallon greater than or less than the price per gallon on March 5?

   _____

3. On March 19, Hector bought 12 gal of gas for $16.68. What was the cost of each gallon of gas? _____

Out for Dinner A group of 13 friends went out for dinner. They decided to share the bill equally.

4. The total bill was $168.35. What was each friend's share? _____

5. After the friends figured a tip, the total amount came to $194.35. What was each friend's share, including tip? _____

6. Because it was Jessica's birthday, the friends decided to treat her and divided the bill 12 ways. To the nearest penny, what would each friend's share of the bill and tip be if only 12 friends contributed? _____

7. **Writing in Math** Eight CDs cost $79.92. Each CD was the same price. What is the cost of each CD? Explain why your answer is logical.

   _____

   _____

   _____

Dividing Decimals by Whole Numbers

Ms. Jenkins's class of 22 students worked together to gather facts about the history of their town. They did library research and interviews with older residents to find their information.

1. Each student wrote an equal amount for the final report. If the entire report was 16.5 pages when printed, what decimal part of a page was contributed by each student?

_____

2. There were 7.7 hr of interviews that were recorded. Each student recorded for an equal amount of time. Did each student tape more or less than a full hour? What decimal part of an hour did each student tape?

_____

The 17 students in wood shop class planned their first project very carefully. The teacher prepared the wood that was needed for the entire class to make coat racks.

3. There was a total length of 105.4 ft of wood for the entire class. In decimal terms, how much lumber did each student get for his or her project?   _____

4. Each student used wooden pegs to make hooks for the coat rack. The pegs were cut from a 212.5 in. length of dowel. Each student received 5 pegs. What was the length of each individual peg?   _____

5. **Writing in Math** Hannah said that if she was given a 5.2-in. dowel rod to make 4 pegs, each would be 13 in. long. Explain Hannah's error. What is the correct answer?

_____

_____

PROBLEM-SOLVING APPLICATIONS

Take Me Out to the Ball Game

Three friends went to see their favorite baseball team play. Each one bought a ticket to the game, a snack, a drink, and a program. Together, the snack, the drink, and the program cost as much as the ticket to the game. The three friends spent a total of $98.04 altogether. How much did the ticket to the game cost?

Read and Understand

1. How much did the three friends spend in total?   _____

2. What are you trying to find?

_____

Plan and Solve

3. What is one hidden question in the problem?

_____

4. Write the answer to the hidden question above.

_____

5. Solve the problem and write your answer in a complete sentence.

_____

Look Back and Check

6. Is your answer reasonable?

_____

_____

Collecting Data from a Survey

Amusement Park Carl took a survey of his eighth-grade class for his project. The survey results are shown on a line plot.

Favorite Amusement Park Ride

		x
	x	x
	x	x
x	x	x
x	x	x
x	x	x
x	x	x
x	x	x
Roller Coaster	Ferris Wheel	Merry-Go-Round

Ride

1. What question might Carl have asked in order to get this information?

   _____

   _____

   _____

   _____

2. How many people responded to this survey?   _____

3. Is the survey question about a fact or an opinion?   _____

4. Write a survey question to gather information on how much time people spend listening to the radio.

   _____

   _____

   _____

5. **Writing in Math** Most of Carl's survey was the result of asking his school friends. Does his survey represent all the people who would go on amusement park rides?

   _____

   _____

   _____

   _____

Name_____

Bar Graphs

Pet Sales A pet store keeps track of its sales each month by the type of animal that is sold. The list shows the number of amphibians and reptiles that were sold in April and May.

Amphibian and Reptile Sales		
	April Sales	May Sales
Frog	17	6
Lizard	5	5
Salamander	7	10
Snake	3	18
Turtle	13	2

1. Complete the graph.

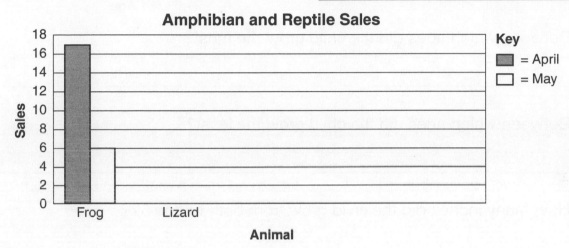

Amphibian and Reptile Sales

Key
■ = April
□ = May

2. How many frogs were sold in April? In May?

_____

3. Which two animals sold better in May than in April?

_____

4. During which month were the greatest number of animals sold? _____

5. **Writing in Math** Rank the animals for the two-month period in order from the least number sold to the greatest number sold. Write the total number sold for each animal. Explain how you determined the ranking.

_____

_____

Line Graphs

Growth A good indication of children's health and nutrition is the rate at which they grow. The graph shows the growth rate of one average healthy child from birth to age 5.

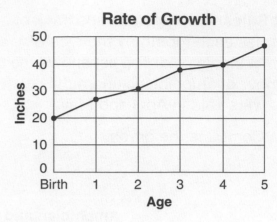

Rate of Growth

1. How tall was the child at age 5?

   _____

2. Between which ages did the child grow the most?

   _____

3. Between which ages did the child grow the least?

   _____

4. How many inches did the child grow from birth to age 5?

   _____

5. Describe the trend shown by the graph. Explain.

   _____

   _____

6. **Writing in Math** Look at the line graph and explain how the line showing the greatest increase in height is different from the line showing the least increase in height.

   _____

   _____

   _____

   _____

Name_____

Stem-and-Leaf Plots

Points Shelly likes to keep track of how many points she scores in each basketball game. The data shows her scores for the games she has played so far this season.

Scores

32	16	22	24
26	36	42	48
18	28	34	36
40	40	16	18
22	20		

1. Complete the stem-and-leaf plot of the data.

Points Scored per Game

Stem	Leaf

2. In how many games did Shelly score 20 or more points?

_____

3. In how many games did Shelly score fewer than 40 points?

_____

4. In how many games did Shelly score at least 40 but less than 49 points?

_____

5. **Writing in Math** Explain why there are two zeros in the leaf following the stem of 4.

_____

_____

_____

Name_____

Make a Graph

Golf Highland High School and Midway High School compete in a golf league. Each game consists of 9 holes. The game winner is the individual student with the lowest score, but the team winner is the team that has the greater number of lower scores. Which school has the greater number of lower scores, Highland or Midway?

Highland High School

Student	1	2	3	4	5	6	7	8
Score	43	51	47	48	41	56	58	47

Midway High School

Student	1	2	3	4	5	6	7	8
Score	41	45	42	59	41	51	42	43

Read and Understand

1. What are you trying to find?

_____

Plan and Solve

2. Complete the stem-and-leaf plots to solve the problem.

Highland			Midway	
Stem	Leaf		Stem	Leaf

3. Write the answer in a complete sentence.

_____

Look Back and Check

4. Is your answer reasonable?

_____

Mean, Median, and Mode

Overtime Bruce works overtime almost every day. Last week he worked 4 hr overtime on Monday, 2 hr on Tuesday, 2 hr on Wednesday, 6 hr on Thursday, and 1 hr on Friday.

1. How many hours overtime did Bruce work the most often? What is this number called?
   _____

2. How many hours overtime did Bruce average last week? What is this number called?
   _____

` 3. What is the median number of hours Bruce worked last week?

Cousins There are 11 first cousins in the Warner family. They love to get together for parties and picnics.

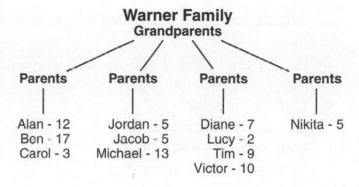

4. What is the name and age of the cousin whose age is the median?

   _____

5. What is the average age of the cousins? Are there any cousins that age?

   _____

6. What age is the most frequent of the cousins? Which cousins are that age?

   _____

7. **Writing in Math** Larry said that the median in a set of data is not important. Give one situation where you could use the median.

   _____

   _____

   _____

Circle Graphs

The circle graph shows the sales of the first 100,000 stuffed animals sold by the Giant Stuffed Animal Company during the first 6 months of the year.

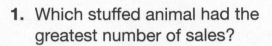

Stuffed Animals

- ■ Dogs
- ▨ Bears
- ▨ Bunnies
- ■ Kangaroos
- ☐ Cats

January–June
100,000 total

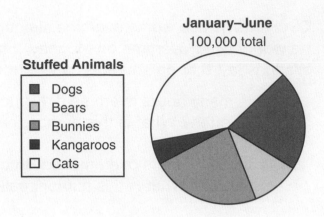

1. Which stuffed animal had the greatest number of sales?

   _____

2. Which had the least number of sales?   _____

3. Which two stuffed animals' sales were the closest?

   _____

4. During the second 6 months of the year, the Olympics were held in Australia and sales of kangaroos soared. Draw a circle graph showing over one half of all sales as kangaroos and the rest evenly distributed between dogs, bears, bunnies, and cats.

5. **Writing in Math** Compare the number of cats sold during the first 6 months of the year with kangaroos sold during the second 6 months of the year. Which was greater? Explain.

   _____

   _____

   _____

   _____

© Pearson Education, Inc. 5

Choosing the Appropriate Graph

Dinner Time Sidney took a survey of his neighbors and his teachers. He asked the survey question, "What time do you normally eat your evening meal?" He graphed the results using a line graph, circle graph, and a line plot.

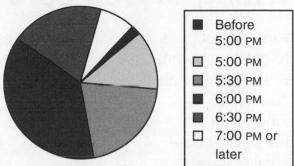

- ■ Before 5:00 PM
- ☐ 5:00 PM
- ▨ 5:30 PM
- ■ 6:00 PM
- ▨ 6:30 PM
- ☐ 7:00 PM or later

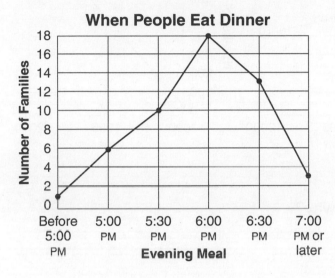

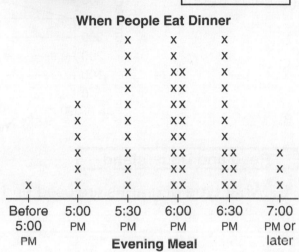

1. At what time do most of the people surveyed eat their evening meal? _____

2. How does each graph show the same result for Exercise 1?

_____

_____

3. Which graph is the least appropriate to use for this survey? Why?

_____

_____

4. **Writing in Math** Which time could be considered the outlier in this survey? Which graph shows you this the best? Why?

_____

_____

Name_____

Writing to Compare

Phone Sales

A telephone company has shown the sales of two types of phones with line graphs. Compare the sales trends.

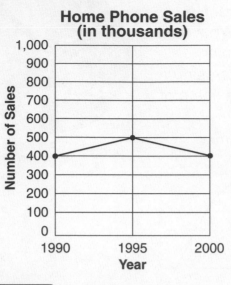

Home Phone Sales (in thousands)

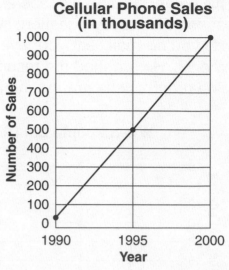

Cellular Phone Sales (in thousands)

Read and Understand

1. What type of graphs are used and why?

_____

_____

Plan and Solve

2. Compare the sales trends.

_____

_____

_____

_____

Look Back and Check

3. Explain why your answer makes sense.

_____

_____

Predicting Outcomes

Gifts Every year the adults in the Anderson family draw names and they each buy a present for that one person. There are 10 adults in the family who participate in this drawing. There are 6 males and 4 females.

1. When drawing a name at random, how many possible outcomes are there? _____

2. Is it equally likely that a male name or a female name will be drawn?

   _____

3. Without looking, a woman draws a name out of a basket. What are her chances of drawing her own name? _____

4. What are her chances of drawing a name other than her own? _____

5. What are her chances of drawing the name of a male? _____

6. What are her chances of drawing the name of a female other than herself? _____

7. **Writing in Math** Rich says that because he is one of the men, he knows that he will draw another man's name. Does he have a better chance to draw a man's name than if a woman drew a name? Explain.

   _____

   _____

   _____

   _____

   _____

Name_____

Listing Outcomes

A coin is tossed 4 times. The coin is equally likely to come up heads or tails.

1. Make a tree diagram to show the sample space.

1st Toss	2nd Toss	3rd Toss	4th Toss

2. What are your chances of tossing 2 tails?

_____

3. **Writing in Math** Melissa says her chances of tossing 3 heads are the same as her chances of tossing 1 tail. Is Melissa correct? Explain.

_____

_____

_____

70 Use with Lesson 5-11.

Expressing Probability as a Fraction

Lucky Ones At a wedding shower, the bride-to-be has placed a mark on the bottom of 3 paper plates. There are 27 guests, and each has a paper plate. The guests who have a mark on their plate get to choose a door prize.

1. Find P(having a marked plate) _____

2. Find P(not having a marked plate) _____

Marbles In a bag, there are 15 blue marbles, 6 red marbles, and 3 white marbles. Sammy draws 1 marble out of the bag.

3. Find P(drawing a red marble) _____

4. Find P(drawing a blue marble) _____

5. Find P(drawing a white marble) _____

6. Find P(not drawing a red marble) _____

7. **Writing in Math** How are the answers for Exercises 3 and 6 related? Explain.

_____

_____

_____

_____

_____

_____

Name_____

Winter Show

The cast members in the winter show wore black shirts and pants, but each was to wear a red or yellow hat, an orange or purple scarf, and green or blue mittens. How many different combinations are there?

Read and Understand

1. What are you trying to find?

_____

Plan and Solve

2. Complete the tree diagram to find the number of combinations.

Hat	Scarf	Mittens	Outcome

R

Y

3. Solve the problem and write the answer in a complete sentence.

_____

Look Back and Check

4. Explain why your answer makes sense.

_____

_____

Geometric Ideas

Spider Webs The intricate web of a spider is a good example
of several geometric concepts. Most spiders begin a web by
spinning 3 strands in the shape of a Y. The spider continues to
add new strands and then connects them in a circular pattern
until it can easily step from one strand onto another.

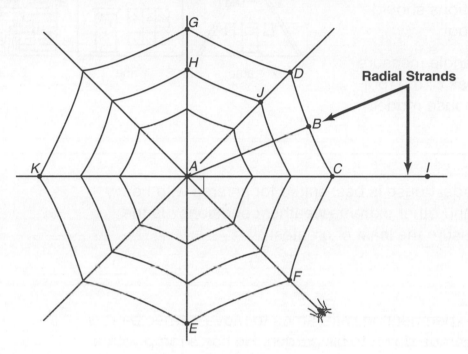

Radial Strands

1. The radial strands that connect the other strands together
   are examples of what geometric concept?

2. Does the spider web have any perpendicular line segments? If so, where?

3. **Writing in Math** Can two lines or line segments be both
   intersecting and parallel? Why or why not?

Name_____

Measuring and Classifying Angles

Roofs Roof designs for houses depend on the weather conditions of an area. A house that is built in an area with heavy snowfall and other extreme weather conditions should have a steep roof.

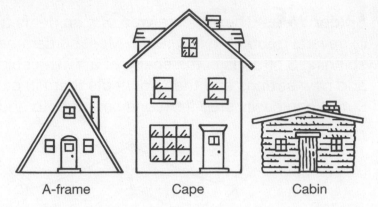

A-frame   Cape   Cabin

1. Give the angle measure for the peak of the roof on each house model.

_____

2. Which model house is best suited for an area with heavy snowfall and other extreme weather conditions? Is the angle measure the least or greatest?

_____

3. Owen is experimenting with ramps to move a wheelbarrow from his garage down to his garden. He has a ramp with a 15° angle and a ramp with a 30° angle. Draw each ramp.

4. **Writing in Math** Savannah says that to change an acute angle to a straight angle, the angle you add will always be an obtuse angle. Is she correct? Explain.

_____

_____

_____

Segments and Angles Related to Circles

Hubcaps Decorative hubcaps add an element of design to any vehicle. Use the hubcap at the right to identify the parts of a circle.

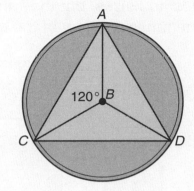

1. What is one line segment that is a chord?

   _____

2. The radius of the hubcap is 7.5 in. What is its diameter?

   _____

3. Part of the design of the hubcap is the circle divided into three equal angles. What is the angle measure of ∠*ABD*?

   _____

4. A flowerpot has a diameter of 8 in. What is its radius?

   _____

5. If a second flowerpot has a radius that is 2 in. greater, what is its diameter?

   _____

6. **Writing in Math** If a circle is divided into 5 sections by 5 radii, and each of the central angles formed are of equal measure, what is the measure of each central angle? Explain how you know.

   _____

   _____

   _____

   _____

   _____

Polygons

Building Blocks A child's building-block set has blocks of all shapes and sizes, but they are all the same thickness. Below are the faces of a few of the blocks.

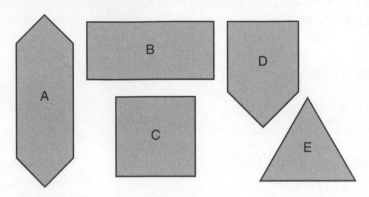

1. Which of the blocks appear to have faces that are regular polygons?

_____

2. Name any two blocks that are the same type of polygon by the number of sides.

_____

The Corral Billy Joe is building an octagonal-shaped corral for his horses. He is making each side 12 ft long.

3. How many sides does the corral have?   _____

4. What is the distance around the corral?   _____

5. **Writing in Math** Explain how you can tell if Billy Joe's corral is a regular polygon.

_____

_____

_____

_____

_____

Classifying Triangles

A patchwork design for quilts is made up of triangles of different shapes, sizes, and colors.

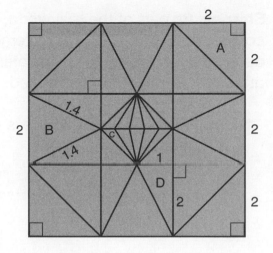

1. Classify triangle A by its sides and angles.

   _____

   _____

2. Classify triangle B by its sides and angles.

   _____

3. Classify triangle C by its sides and angles.

   _____

4. Classify triangle D by its sides and angles.

   _____

5. Jacob took three sticks that were each 7 in. long. He formed a triangle with the sticks, with the tips of each stick touching another. What is the measure of each of the angles?

   _____

   _____

6. **Writing in Math** Mindy says that if a triangle has two angles that are both 42°, the triangle is an acute triangle. Is she right? Explain your answer.

   _____

   _____

   _____

   _____

Classifying Quadrilaterals

Shapes As part of the real world, there are many things that could be identified as quadrilaterals. Their angles and sides determine what type of quadrilateral they are. For each quadrilateral shown or described, tell the geometric name.

1. The shape of the necklace is what type of quadrilateral?

_____

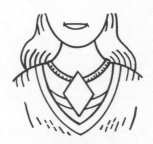

2. The shape of the shaded part of the frame of the doorway is what type of quadrilateral?

_____

3. The shape of the baseball diamond is what type of quadrilateral?

_____

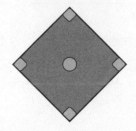

4. **Writing in Math** The qualities of a square match the definition of two types of parallelograms. Name both and explain the characteristics for each definition.

_____

_____

_____

_____

Name_____

Solve a Simpler Problem

School Work Margaret's older brother has given her a problem that he is sure will stump her. He wants to know the sum of the angles of a 32-sided regular polygon. Margaret knows that a triangle has 180°, a quadrilateral has 360° and can be divided into 2 triangles, and a pentagon can be divided into 3 triangles. What is the answer to her brother's problem?

Read and Understand

1. What are you trying to find?

_____

Plan and Solve

2. Complete the table.

Sides in a Polygon	3	4	5	6	7	8	. . .	32
Number of Triangles	1	2	3					
Sum of Angles	180°	360°	540°					

3. Solve the simpler problem by seeing a pattern and completing a calculation.

_____

_____

4. Use the answers to the simpler problem to solve the original problem.

_____

Look Back and Check

5. Is your work correct? Explain how you checked your answer.

_____

_____

Name_____

Writing to Describe

Birdbath Nancy asked her family to buy her a birdbath. There were two similar birdbaths at the store, so she needs to describe it very carefully. Use geometric terms to describe the birdbath that Nancy wants to buy.

Birdbath A   Nancy likes this one.

Top view   **Side view**

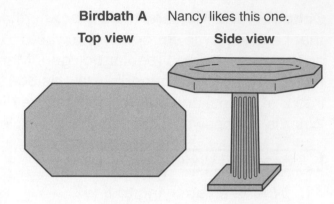

Read and Understand

1. What are you trying to describe?

_____

_____

Birdbath B

Top view   **Side view**

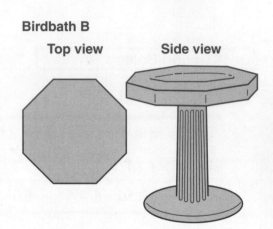

Plan and Solve

2. What is a geometric characteristic of the top shape of the birdbath that Nancy wants?

_____

_____

3. What is a geometric characteristic of the bottom shape of the birdbath that Nancy wants?

_____

4. Write the description of the birdbath Nancy wants in a complete sentence.

_____

Look Back and Check

5. Explain how you can check your answer.

_____

Congruence and Similarity

Binoculars A pair of binoculars has a magnification of 6 times the actual viewing size.

1. Will the item viewed through the binoculars be congruent to the item viewed with the naked eye? _____

2. Will it be similar? _____

3. If an object is actually an inch and a half tall, how tall should the image appear to be when you look through the binoculars? _____

Flags American flags are made in many sizes for ceremonies and everyday display. Two of the most commonly sold sizes are shown.

4. Are the two flags congruent?

_____

5. Are the two flags similar? _____

6. **Writing in Math** One of the more popular sizes for flags flown at government buildings has a width of 20 ft. If the flag is going to be similar to the other two, what should the length of the flag be? Explain how you found the answer.

_____

_____

_____

_____

_____

_____

Name_____

Transformations

Photography Susan is learning photography and has made a mistake. When she developed her film, she printed the image with the film upside down, which caused the print to be made in the back of the negative.

1. What type of transformation is Susan's print?

_____

2. Susan had taken a photo of Jim, who had a freckle under his left eye. Because of Susan's mistake, under which eye did the freckle appear in the photo?

_____

Marching In marching drills the command right-face is a 90° turn to the right, left-face is a 90° turn to the left, and about-face is a 180° turn to the right.

3. The drill team enters a stadium facing north. They are given the commands left-face, about-face, and right-face as they march. What direction will they be facing at the end of the drill?

_____

4. Since the team has been marching straight ahead as well as turning, what transformations will have occurred to their formation?

_____

5. **Writing in Math** When a transformation of a slide, a flip, or a turn is performed, is the resulting image congruent or similar to the original? Explain.

_____

_____

_____

Symmetry

1. Complete the drawings using the dotted line as the line of symmetry.

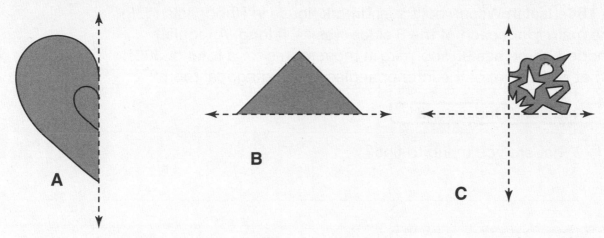

A   B   C

2. How many lines of symmetry does figure A have?

_____

3. Does figure B have a second line of symmetry?

_____

4. A square has a horizontal and a vertical line of symmetry.
   What is a third line of symmetry?

_____

_____

5. **Writing in Math** Explain how symmetry and a flip transformation are alike.

_____

_____

_____

_____

_____

Name_____

Octagon House

In 1844 Isaiah Wilcox built a landmark house in Rhode Island. In the main room each of the 8 sides was 17 ft long. A regularly shaped home has 90° corners in most rooms for a total of 360°. What is the sum of the interior angles in an octagonal room?

Read and Understand

1. What are you trying to find?

_____

Plan and Solve

2. Break apart or change the problem(s) into one that is simpler to solve.

_____

_____

3. Solve the simpler problem(s).

_____

4. Use the answers to the simpler problem to solve the original problem.

_____

_____

Look Back and Check

5. Explain how you can check your answer.

_____

_____

Meanings of Fractions

Names of Days The table shows the days of the week categorized by the number of letters in their names.

Number of Letters in Names of Days

Number of Letters	Names of Days	Number of Days in Week with Given Number of Letters
6	Sunday, Monday, Friday	3
7	Tuesday	1
8	Thursday, Saturday	2
9	Wednesday	1

1. Write the fraction that names the number of days in the week that have a total of 6 letters. _____

2. Write the fraction that names the number of days in the week that have a total of 7 letters. _____

3. Write the fraction that names the number of days in the week that have a total of 8 letters. _____

4. Write the fraction that names the number of days in the week that have a total of 9 letters. _____

5. **Writing in Math** The fraction $\frac{3}{7}$ is made of two parts. Use the chart above to explain what the numerator and the denominator represent.

_____

_____

_____

_____

_____

Fractions and Division

An analog clock has a face with a set of numbers and an hour and a minute hand.

1. Based on the number of hours, how many equal sections are on the clock?

   _____

2. What part of the whole clock is shown by the shaded section?

   _____

Nurses often spend their time performing different tasks. They also often work in 12 hr shifts.

3. The clock shows how many hours in one 12 hr shift a nurse spent checking on patients. Write a fraction that shows this information.

   _____

4. The clock shows how many hours in one 12 hr shift a nurse spent on paperwork. Write a fraction that shows this information.

   _____

5. **Writing in Math** If a nurse spent 2 hr of one shift and 2 hr of another shift on paperwork, what fraction of one 12-hr period did he or she spend on paperwork? Explain your answer.

   _____

   _____

   _____

Mixed Numbers

Mineral water is a very popular drink in the United States and all over the world. Mineral water is often sold in 6-bottle packs.

1. Suppose you have 11 bottles of mineral water. Write the number of 6-bottle packs you have as a mixed number.

   _____

2. Suppose you have two 6-bottle packs of mineral water. Write the number of 6-bottle packs you have as an improper fraction.

   _____

3. Suppose you have 15 bottles of mineral water. Write the number of 6-bottle packs you have as both a mixed number and an improper fraction.

   _____

Betty bought a photo album to put some pictures in. Each page of the album holds 4 photos.

4. If Betty has 14 photos she wants to put in the album, how many pages can she fill? Write your answer as an improper fraction.

   _____

5. If Betty has 25 photos she wants to put in the album, how many pages can she fill? Write your answer as a mixed number.

   _____

6. **Writing in Math** If Betty filled $6\frac{3}{4}$ pages of the album with photos, how many photos did she put in the album? Explain how changing $6\frac{3}{4}$ to an improper fraction helps you find the answer.

   _____

   _____

   _____

   _____

Estimating Fractional Amounts

Tall Trees There are four tall trees in Lisa's backyard. The picture shows the heights of the trees.

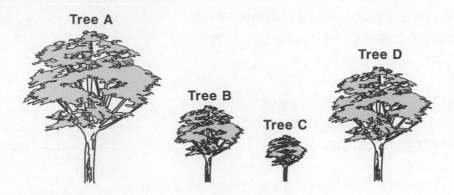

Tree A

Tree D

Tree B

Tree C

1. Using a benchmark fraction, estimate how tall Tree B is compared to Tree A. _____

2. Using a benchmark fraction, estimate how tall Tree C is compared to Tree A. _____

3. Using a benchmark fraction, estimate how tall Tree D is compared to Tree A. _____

4. Using a benchmark fraction, estimate how tall Tree C is compared to Tree B. _____

5. Using a benchmark fraction, estimate how tall Tree B is compared to Tree D. _____

6. **Writing in Math** Are benchmark fractions helpful to use with numbers greater than 1? Explain.

_____

_____

_____

_____

_____

Fractions and Mixed Numbers on the Number Line

Free Throws Gail is on the basketball team. Every week after school, she shoots 20 free throws in practice. The chart shows the number of free throws out of 20 she made each day last week.

Day	Free Throws Made/Attempted
Monday	$\frac{16}{20}$
Tuesday	$\frac{11}{20}$
Wednesday	$\frac{9}{20}$
Thursday	$\frac{19}{20}$
Friday	$\frac{14}{20}$

1. On the number line, show the fractions that represent how many free throws Gail made out of 20.

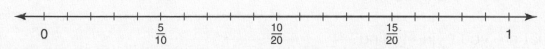

2. Now write the fractions in order from least to greatest.

_____

3. Carly, Morris, and Becky went to a book fair. Carly spent $\frac{5}{9}$ of her weekly allowance, Morris spent $1\frac{2}{9}$, and Becky spent $\frac{25}{9}$. Write the fractions in order on the number line. If each receives the same allowance, who spent the greatest amount?

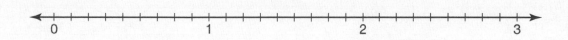

_____

4. **Writing in Math** Explain how you would set up a number line to compare $\frac{5}{12}$, $2\frac{7}{12}$, $1\frac{1}{12}$, and $\frac{11}{12}$.

_____

_____

_____

Extra or Missing Information

Rental Car Mr. Bertram rented a car for $225.00 per week. He was given 250 free miles for the week and had to pay $0.10 for each extra mile. When Mr. Bertram returned the car, he paid an additional $23.50 for extra mileage. How much did the rental car cost Mr. Bertram?

Read and Understand

1. How much would Mr. Bertram pay if he drove less than 250 mi?   _____

2. How much extra did Mr. Bertram pay for driving more than 250 mi?   _____

3. What are you trying to find?

_____

Plan and Solve

4. Is there enough information to solve the problem?   _____

5. Is there information you do not need to solve the problem? What is it?

_____

_____

6. Solve the problem. Write your answer in a complete sentence.

_____

Look Back and Check

7. Is your answer correct?

_____

Name_____

Understanding Equivalent Fractions

Everglades National Park Everglades National Park in southern Florida is home to thousands of wildlife creatures. The park has changed as people have used water for other purposes. The Florida panther has become an endangered species. In 2002, experts estimated that there are only about 30 Florida panthers living in Florida. They also estimated that only about 10 of the panthers were living in the Everglades.

1. Write a fraction that compares the estimated number of Florida panthers in the Everglades to the total estimated number of Florida panthers in Florida.   _____

2. What is an equivalent fraction for the fraction you found in Exercise 1?   _____

3. Find the equivalent fraction for $\frac{1}{3}$ that has a denominator of 6. Draw fraction strips to show why they are equivalent.   _____

4. Suppose 10 new panthers were discovered in Florida, and they were not in the Everglades. What fraction would compare the estimated number of Florida panthers living in the Everglades to the total estimated number of Florida panthers in Florida? Also write an equivalent fraction for your answer.   _____

5. **Writing in Math** Is $\frac{5}{8}$ an equivalent fraction for $\frac{2}{3}$? Explain how you can tell using fraction strips.

_____

_____

_____

Name_____

Equivalent Fractions

Many scientists believe that dinosaurs ruled the Earth millions of years ago. Today, the only evidence we have of these reptiles comes from fossils that are discovered in different parts of the world.

1. A giraffe is about $\frac{1}{3}$ the size of the average *Brachiosaurus* dinosaur. Find the equivalent fraction for $\frac{1}{3}$ with a denominator of 9.   _____

2. Now find the equivalent fraction for $\frac{1}{3}$ with a numerator of 5.   _____

3. Is $\frac{10}{30}$ equivalent to $\frac{1}{3}$?   _____

4. An average adult human's height is about $\frac{1}{4}$ the height of a *Tyrannosaurus rex.* Find the equivalent fraction for $\frac{1}{4}$ with a denominator of 20.   _____

5. Now find the equivalent fraction for $\frac{1}{4}$ with a numerator of 3.   _____

6. Is $\frac{5}{25}$ equivalent to $\frac{1}{4}$?   _____

7. A *Stegosaurus*'s height was about $\frac{3}{10}$ of its length. Find the equivalent fraction for $\frac{3}{10}$ with a denominator of 30.   _____

8. Find an equivalent fraction for $\frac{3}{10}$ that has a numerator of 12.   _____

9. Is $\frac{18}{60}$ equivalent to $\frac{3}{10}$?   _____

10. **Writing in Math** Explain how you found your answer to Exercise 6.

_____

_____

_____

Greatest Common Factor

Life expectancy is the average number of years a person lives. In 2002, the life expectancy of a male in Japan was about 78 years. The life expectancy for a female was about 84 years.

1. What are the factors of 78? Of 84?

_____

_____

_____

_____

2. What are the common factors of 78 and 84? _____

3. What is the greatest common factor of 78 and 84? _____

In 2002, about 15 out of every 100 Japanese citizens were 14 years or younger. In China, about 25 out of every 100 Chinese citizens were 14 years or younger.

4. What are the factors of 15? Of 25?

_____

5. What are the common factors of 15 and 25? _____

6. What is the greatest common factor of 15 and 25? _____

7. **Writing in Math** Is 10 a factor of 15 or 25? Explain how you know.

_____

_____

_____

Fractions in Simplest Form

Student Survey In 2002, a national survey of students was conducted in the United States. The students responded to many different questions, including the color of their favorite school uniform, as well as questions about the United States.

1. Out of every 100 students, about 16 said they thought the U.S. government was doing enough to protect the environment. What is the greatest common factor of 16 and 100? _____

2. What is $\frac{16}{100}$ in simplest form? _____

3. Out of every 100 students, about 84 said they thought the U.S. government was not doing enough to protect the environment. What is the greatest common factor of 84 and 100? _____

4. What is $\frac{84}{100}$ in simplest form? _____

5. Of the students who said they thought the U.S. government was doing enough, about 36 out of every 100 students was a girl. What is $\frac{36}{100}$ in simplest form? _____

6. Of the students who said they thought the U.S. government was doing enough, about 64 out of every 100 students was a boy. What is $\frac{64}{100}$ in simplest form? _____

7. **Writing in Math** Explain how you know $\frac{11}{13}$ is in simplest form.

_____

_____

_____

_____

_____

Name_____

Understanding Comparing Fractions

Dog Food Diet is an important part of keeping a dog healthy. One dog food company supplied information for how much dry and canned food to feed a "senior" dog that is 7 years old or older. The amount of each type of dog food depends on the weight of the dog. Use the fraction strips to complete Exercises 1–3. Write >, <, or = for each _____ .

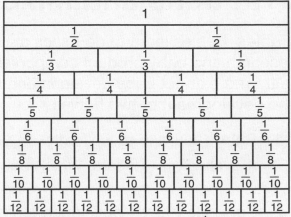

1. One weight class of senior dogs should eat no more than about $\frac{1}{2}$ c of dry food each day. Another weight class of senior dogs should eat no more than about $\frac{7}{8}$ c of dry food each day. Compare the amounts.

   $\frac{1}{2}$ _____ $\frac{7}{8}$

2. A 10 lb senior dog should eat about $\frac{3}{8}$ c of dry food and about $\frac{1}{3}$ can of canned food each day. Compare the amounts.

   $\frac{3}{8}$ _____ $\frac{1}{3}$

3. A 20 lb senior dog should eat about $\frac{2}{3}$ c of dry food and about $\frac{4}{6}$ can of canned food each day. Compare the amounts.

   $\frac{2}{3}$ _____ $\frac{4}{6}$

Reading Over the weekend, Craig, Dottie, and Hale started reading the same book. Craig read $\frac{1}{2}$ of the book, Dottie read $\frac{5}{8}$ of the book, and Hale read $\frac{2}{5}$ of the book.

4. Who read more, Craig or Hale? _____

5. Who read more, Craig or Dottie? _____

6. Who read more, Dottie or Hale? _____

7. **Writing in Math** Explain why Craig's having read $\frac{1}{2}$ the book makes it easier to compare who read more.

_____

_____

Comparing and Ordering Fractions and Mixed Numbers

Babies Babies learn to do things at different ages. Medical research and baby product companies often conduct studies to learn more about baby development. Suppose a group studied the development of two babies.

1. Baby 1 learned to walk after $1\frac{1}{4}$ years. Baby 2 learned to walk after $\frac{19}{12}$ years. Which baby walked first? _____

2. Suppose Baby 1 developed teeth after $\frac{1}{2}$ year and Baby 2 developed teeth after $\frac{5}{12}$ years. Which baby developed teeth first? _____

3. Suppose Baby 1 learned to point to the eyes, ears, and nose after $2\frac{1}{3}$ years. Baby 2 learned to do it after $2\frac{5}{12}$ years. Which baby learned first? _____

Rock Collections Edward and Steven collect rocks. Edward's rocks are $1\frac{3}{4}$, $2\frac{7}{9}$, $2\frac{5}{6}$, and $1\frac{2}{5}$ in. long. Steven's rocks are $2\frac{3}{5}$, $1\frac{4}{7}$, $2\frac{1}{2}$, and $1\frac{5}{8}$ in. long.

4. Order Edward's collection from least to greatest.

_____

5. Order Steven's collection from least to greatest.

_____

6. **Writing in Math** How can you tell that $\frac{4}{7}$ is greater than $\frac{1}{2}$ without finding a common denominator?

_____

_____

_____

Fractions and Decimals

Budgets Every state must carefully track the income it receives and the money it spends. This data is usually found in a state's annual budget. The chart shows the state income for Arkansas in 2000.

2000 Arkansas Income Report

Income Source	Fraction or Decimal Amount of Total State Income
General revenues	$\frac{38}{100}$
Federal funds	0.250
Special revenues	$\frac{80}{1,000}$
Cash funds	0.060
Trust funds	$\frac{18}{100}$
Other	0.050

1. General revenues were $\frac{38}{100}$ of the state's income. Write $\frac{38}{100}$ as a decimal.

   _____

2. Federal funds were 0.250 of the state's income. Write 0.250 as a fraction. _____

3. Special revenues were $\frac{80}{1,000}$ of the state's income. Write $\frac{80}{1,000}$ as a decimal. _____

4. Cash funds were 0.060 of the state's income. Write 0.060 as a fraction.

5. Trust funds were $\frac{18}{100}$ of the state's income. Write $\frac{18}{100}$ as a decimal. _____

6. Funds from other sources were 0.050 of the state's income. Write 0.050 as a fraction. _____

7. **Writing in Math** Explain why you can use division to convert a fraction to a decimal.

   _____

   _____

   _____

   _____

Fractions and Decimals on the Number Line

Greg, Donna, and Pat went fishing. Each caught three fish. The fish Greg caught weighed $1\frac{3}{10}$ lb, $1\frac{3}{8}$ lb, and 1.2 lb. The fish Donna caught weighed 1.8 lb, $1\frac{3}{5}$ lb, and 1.2 lb. The fish Pat caught weighed $1\frac{4}{8}$ lb, 1.4 lb, and $\frac{2}{3}$ lb.

1. Show the weights of Greg's fish on the number line.

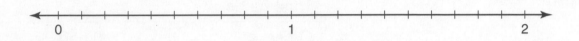

2. What was the greatest weight of the fish Greg caught? _____

3. Show the weights of Donna's fish on the number line.

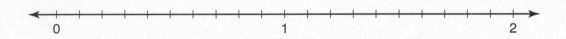

4. What was the greatest weight of the fish Donna caught? _____

5. Show the weights of Pat's fish on the number line.

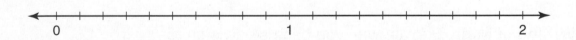

6. What was the greatest weight of the fish Pat caught? _____

7. **Writing in Math** Explain how placing numbers on a number line can help you find which number is greatest or least.

_____

_____

Name_____

Use Logical Reasoning

Capitals Venezuela, Argentina, Chile, and Colombia are four
countries in South America. Their capital cities are Santiago,
Bogotá, Caracas, and Buenos Aires, but not necessarily in that
order. If you know that Caracas is the capital of Venezuela, that
Santiago is not the capital of Argentina, and that Bogotá is the
capital of Colombia, then what are the capitals of each country?

Read and Understand

1. What two capitals do you know?

   _____

2. What are you trying to find?   _____

Plan and Solve

3. What strategy will you use?   _____

4. Complete the chart to help solve the problem.

	Santiago	Bogotá	Caracas	Buenos Aires
Venezuela				
Argentina				
Chile				
Colombia				

5. Solve the problem. Write your answer in a complete sentence.

   _____

   _____

   _____

Look Back and Check

6. Is your work reasonable?   _____

Name_____

Groceries

Ms. Whitworth bought groceries for $67.25. She received
$12.75 in change from the cashier. Ms. Whitworth had $100.00
in her purse. How much money did she give the cashier?

Read and Understand

1. How much did the groceries cost?   _____

2. How much change did Ms. Whitworth receive? _____

3. What are you trying to find?

_____

_____

Plan and Solve

4. Is there enough information to solve the problem? _____

5. Is there information you do not need to solve the problem? What is it?

_____

_____

6. Solve the problem.

_____

7. Write the answer in a complete sentence.

_____

Look Back and Check

8. Is your answer correct?

_____

Name_____

Adding and Subtracting Fractions with Like Denominators

Gold Gold is a very valuable mineral that is measured in units called troy ounces.

1. Suppose a jeweler uses $\frac{7}{12}$ troy ounces to produce a ring and $\frac{11}{12}$ troy ounces to produce a set of earrings. How many total troy ounces did the jeweler use? _____

2. In Exercise 1, how many more troy ounces did the jeweler use for the earrings than for the ring?

_____

3. Suppose a jeweler makes a ring that is made of $\frac{7}{8}$ troy ounces of gold. Then the jeweler makes a second ring that has $\frac{3}{8}$ troy ounces of gold. How many total troy ounces did the jeweler use? _____

4. In Exercise 3, how many more troy ounces did the jeweler use for the first ring than the second ring?

_____

Where Is the Gold? Gold can be found in 40 of the 50 U.S. states. Only 22 states produce gold commercially.

5. Suppose 3 states produce $\frac{7}{16}$ of the gold in the United States each year. Suppose 7 other states produce $\frac{3}{16}$ of the gold. What fraction of the gold produced in the United States each year comes from these 10 states?

_____

6. **Writing in Math** In Exercise 5, what fraction of the gold is produced by the other states? Explain how you found your answer.

_____

Name _____

Understanding Adding and Subtracting with Unlike Denominators

Bat Facts Bats are the only mammals in the animal kingdom that can fly. The brown bat reaches an adult wingspan of about 13 to 14 in. The biggest bat in the state of Oregon is the hoary bat, which weighs about 1 oz. For 1–6, you may use fraction strips or draw pictures to help.

1. Suppose a baby brown bat has a wingspan that is $\frac{1}{6}$ of its adult wingspan. Then the bat's wingspan grows another $\frac{1}{4}$ of its adult wingspan. What fraction of its adult wingspan has it reached?

   _____

2. Is it correct to say that the bat in Exercise 1 has reached $\frac{1}{2}$ of its adult wingspan after the second growth period? _____

3. Suppose one hoary bat weighs $\frac{7}{12}$ oz and a second hoary bat weighs $\frac{3}{4}$ oz. Which bat weighs more? _____

4. What do the bats in Exercise 3 weigh altogether? _____

5. How much lighter is the lighter bat in Exercise 3 than the heavier bat? _____

6. What would be the total weight of two bats that weighed $\frac{1}{2}$ and $\frac{1}{3}$ of an ounce? _____

7. **Writing in Math** Which fractions would be easier to add, $\frac{1}{6} + \frac{1}{3}$ or $\frac{1}{5} + \frac{1}{2}$? Explain.

   _____

   _____

   _____

   _____

Least Common Denominator

Snack Time Carlos has a snack every day after he gets home from school. On Tuesday his snack was a small bag of carrots. He ate $\frac{1}{3}$ of the bag before doing his homework and $\frac{3}{7}$ of the bag after finishing his homework.

1. What is the LCM of 3 and 7? _____

2. What is the LCD of $\frac{1}{3}$ and $\frac{3}{7}$? _____

3. How much of the bag of carrots
   did Carlos eat altogether? _____

Schedule Over the weekend Vicki spends $\frac{2}{9}$ of her free time visiting with family, $\frac{1}{6}$ doing chores, $\frac{1}{5}$ playing with friends, and $\frac{3}{8}$ doing homework.

4. What is the LCD of the fraction of time Vicki
   spends visiting with family and doing chores? _____

5. What is the LCD of the fraction of time Vicki
   spends playing with friends and doing homework? _____

6. What is the LCD of the fraction of time Vicki
   spends visiting with family and playing
   with friends? _____

7. What is the LCD of the fraction of time Vicki
   spends doing homework and doing chores? _____

8. What is the LCD of the fraction of time Vicki
   spends doing chores and playing with friends? _____

9. What is the LCD of the fraction of time Vicki
   spends doing homework and visiting with family? _____

10. **Writing in Math** Victor said that it is not always necessary to find
    the LCD to compare the sizes of fractions. Do you agree? Explain.

_____

_____

Adding and Subtracting Fractions with Unlike Denominators

Lunch Jesse, Veronica, Sal, and Juanita went out to lunch for pizza. Jesse ate $\frac{3}{10}$ of a pizza, Veronica ate $\frac{1}{4}$ of a pizza, Sal ate $\frac{3}{8}$ of a pizza, and Juanita ate $\frac{1}{3}$ of a pizza.

1. How much did Jesse and Veronica eat altogether?   _____

2. How much did Sal and Veronica eat altogether?   _____

3. How much did Jesse, Sal, and Veronica eat altogether?   _____

4. How much did Veronica, Juanita, and Jesse eat altogether?   _____

Teachers Look at the data for the fraction of Illinois teachers with graduate degrees.

Fraction of Total Public School Teachers in Illinois

	1991	1996	2001
Teachers with Graduate Degrees	$\frac{9}{20}$	$\frac{11}{25}$	$\frac{47}{100}$

5. What is the difference between the fraction of teachers with graduate degrees in 2001 and 1996?   _____

6. What is the difference between the number of teachers with graduate degrees in 2001 and 1991?   _____

7. **Writing in Math** Louisa says that if you add fractions using the LCD, you will never have to simplify the answer. Is she correct? Explain.

_____

_____

_____

_____

Understanding Adding and Subtracting Mixed Numbers

Growth Spurt Usually, the weight of a human baby doubles within the first four months of life and then triples by the end of the first year. Suppose a baby gains $2\frac{1}{6}$ lb in the first month and $1\frac{5}{6}$ lb in the second month. For 1–3, you may use fraction strips or draw pictures to help.

1. How much weight did the baby gain in the first two months?
   _____

2. How much more weight did the baby gain in the first month than the second month?
   _____

3. Suppose the baby gains another $1\frac{5}{6}$ lb in the third month. How much weight has the baby gained in the first three months?
   _____

A Swim in the Lake On vacation, the Simon family likes to go swimming in the lake. One day, Rebecca swam for $1\frac{2}{5}$ hr, Paul swam for $1\frac{4}{5}$ hr, Lydia swam for $2\frac{2}{5}$ hr, and Nathan swam for a full 3 hr. For 4–6, you may use fraction strips or draw pictures to help.

4. How long did Rebecca and Lydia swim in total?
   _____

5. How much longer did Lydia swim than Paul?
   _____

6. How much longer did Nathan swim than Paul?
   _____

7. **Writing in Math** Did Rebecca and Paul in total swim longer than Nathan did? Explain how you found your answer.

   _____

   _____

   _____

Estimating Sums and Differences of Mixed Numbers

Three Trees Three trees in Melissa's yard are $8\frac{1}{3}$, $11\frac{4}{7}$, and $13\frac{6}{11}$ ft high. Find estimates for 1–4.

1. About how tall are the two shorter trees combined?

   _____

2. About how tall are the two taller trees combined?

   _____

3. About how tall are the shortest and tallest trees combined?

   _____

4. About how tall are all three trees combined? _____

Lace 'Em Up In a school basketball game, Larry plays $2\frac{1}{8}$ quarters, P. J. plays $2\frac{3}{5}$ quarters, and Maurice plays $3\frac{3}{4}$ quarters. Find estimates for 5–7.

5. About how many more quarters did P. J. play than Larry?

   _____

6. About how many more quarters did Maurice play than Larry?

   _____

7. About how many more quarters did Maurice play than P. J.?

   _____

8. **Writing in Math** If P. J. had played half more of a quarter, would your answer to Exercise 7 change? Explain.

   _____

   _____

Name_____

Adding Mixed Numbers

Jill's Day On Friday, Jill's mother drove her to school. After school, they drove to the library to check out a book and then to the grocery store to shop. Afterward, they drove home. The distances between each location are shown on the drawing. The arrows show the direction of the route Jill and her mother took.

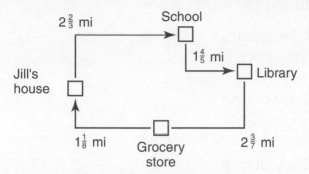

1. Jill and her mother drove from Jill's house to school, then they drove to the library. How far did they drive? _____

2. How far was the drive from the school to the grocery store? _____

3. How far was the drive from the library to home? _____

Meals in Space Because of limited space, astronauts can only eat so much food each day. Suppose a space shuttle astronaut eats about $2\frac{3}{5}$ lb of food each day and that the packaging weighs $1\frac{1}{8}$ lb. Also suppose that an astronaut eats a total of $7\frac{1}{3}$ lb of meat and $5\frac{3}{4}$ lb of vegetables in one week.

4. What is the combined weight of the food an astronaut eats each day and its packaging? _____

5. What is the combined weight of the meat and vegetables an astronaut eats each week? _____

6. **Writing in Math** Find an estimate for the answer to Exercise 3. Is your exact answer reasonable? Explain.

_____

_____

Subtracting Mixed Numbers

Thirsty Corn Corn is one of the main farming products in the state of Iowa. As you might guess, rain is very important to the farming industry in Iowa. Suppose in Sibley, Iowa, there was a total of $1\frac{7}{12}$ in. of rain during the second week of July, $3\frac{1}{12}$ in. during the third week, and $3\frac{5}{8}$ in. during the fourth week.

1. How much more rain fell in Sibley during the third week than the second week? _____

2. How much more rain fell in Sibley during the fourth week than the second week? _____

3. How much more rain fell in Sibley during the fourth week than the third week? _____

Soccer Allisa, Kay, and Fran played in a game of soccer on a hot day. During the game, Allisa drank $2\frac{3}{5}$ glasses of water, Kay drank 4 glasses of water, and Fran drank $3\frac{1}{6}$ glasses of water.

4. How much more water did Kay drink than Allisa? _____

5. How much more water did Kay drink than Fran? _____

6. How much more water did Fran drink than Allisa? _____

7. **Writing in Math** Explain why you had to rename the number 4 twice to solve the exercises in the Soccer problem.

_____

_____

_____

_____

PROBLEM-SOLVING STRATEGY PS 8-9

Work Backward

Fuel Mark kept track of the amount of gasoline his car used for 3 days. On the first day, $3\frac{1}{5}$ gal were used. On the second day, $4\frac{1}{4}$ gal were used. On the third day, $2\frac{7}{10}$ gal were used and $1\frac{1}{2}$ gal were left in the tank. How many gallons of gasoline did Mark's car have at the beginning of the 3-day period?

Read and Understand

1. How many gallons of gasoline were used each day?

   _____

2. How many gallons of gasoline were left after 3 days? _____

3. What are you trying to find?

   _____

   _____

Plan and Solve

4. What strategy will you use? _____

5. Write and solve an equation to solve the problem. Write your answer in a complete sentence.

   _____

   _____

   _____

Look Back and Check

6. Is your answer reasonable?

   _____

Multiplying Fractions by Whole Numbers

Model Your Money For 1–3, shade the pictures to help you find the answers.

1. Suppose you have 15 $1 bills. You use $\frac{1}{5}$ of the $1 bills to buy a book. How many $1 bills did you use?

_____

2. Suppose you have 16 quarters. You use $\frac{3}{8}$ of the quarters to buy 2 cans of juice. How many quarters did you use?

_____

3. Suppose you have nine $5 bills. You use $\frac{1}{3}$ of the $5 bills to buy 2 CDs. How much did you pay for the 2 CDs?

_____

4. **Writing in Math** Explain how you could use mental math to find $\frac{3}{10}$ of 30.

_____

_____

Name_____

Estimating Products of Fractions

Heave It Brett can throw a football farther than any of his friends. His best throw measured 96 ft. For 1–4, estimate each product.

1. Craig can throw a football $\frac{4}{7}$ of the distance Brett can. About how far can Craig throw a football?

_____

2. Fred can throw a football $\frac{9}{13}$ of the distance Brett can throw a football. About how far can Fred throw a football?

_____

3. Sergio can throw a football $\frac{7}{9}$ of the distance Brett can throw a football. About how far can Sergio throw a football?

_____

Commute In one week, Mr. Jansen drove 48 mi total in 10 trips to and from work.

4. About how many miles did Mr. Jansen drive in 4 trips? Use a benchmark fraction to find your answer.

_____

5. About how many miles did Mr. Jansen drive in 7 trips? Use compatible numbers to find your answer.

_____

6. **Writing in Math** Did you use a benchmark fraction or compatible numbers for Exercise 3? Explain.

_____

_____

_____

_____

Name _____

Multiplying Fractions

Cantaloupes Michelle went shopping with her dad. They bought 4 cantaloupes, the largest of which weighed $\frac{7}{8}$ lb. For 1–3, simplify your answer, if necessary.

1. If the smallest cantaloupe weighed $\frac{1}{2}$ as much as the largest cantaloupe, how much did it weigh?   _____

2. If another of the cantaloupes weighed $\frac{5}{7}$ as much as the largest cantaloupe, how much did it weigh?   _____

3. If another of the cantaloupes weighed $\frac{7}{9}$ as much as the largest cantaloupe, how much did it weigh?   _____

Nature Trail The nature trail at a park near Justin's home is $\frac{3}{4}$ mi. There are many interesting stops along the way. For 4–5, simplify your answer, if necessary.

4. There is a hill that offers great views $\frac{1}{3}$ of the way from the beginning of the trail. How many miles is the walk to the hill?   _____

5. A stream that Justin likes to soak his feet in is $\frac{5}{8}$ of the way from the beginning of the trail. How many miles is the walk to the stream?   _____

6. **Writing in Math** Explain how you could use a piece of paper to model the problem $\frac{1}{3} \times \frac{2}{3}$.

_____

_____

_____

_____

_____

Multiplying Mixed Numbers

Sandcastles Yvonne, Manny, Raul, and Beatrice were building sandcastles at the beach. They were trying to see who could build the tallest sandcastle. Beatrice's sandcastle was $1\frac{3}{5}$ ft tall.

1. Yvonne's sandcastle was $1\frac{1}{4}$ times as tall as Beatrice's. What is $1\frac{1}{4} \times 1\frac{3}{5}$ ft? _____

2. Manny's sandcastle was $1\frac{2}{3}$ times as tall as Beatrice's. What is $1\frac{2}{3} \times 1\frac{3}{5}$ ft? _____

3. Raul's sandcastle was $2\frac{1}{8}$ times as tall as Beatrice's. What is $2\frac{1}{8} \times 1\frac{3}{5}$ ft? _____

Land Measures Land areas are often measured in square sections or units. One common land measure is an **acre**. An acre was once defined as the amount of land a pair of oxen could plow in one day. Today, a square acre of land measures about 209 feet on each side.

4. Suppose an area of land Is $3\frac{1}{4}$ sections long and $2\frac{7}{8}$ sections wide. What is $3\frac{1}{4} \times 2\frac{7}{8}$? _____

5. Suppose an area of land is $5\frac{1}{5}$ sections long and $4\frac{5}{6}$ sections wide. What is $5\frac{1}{5} \times 4\frac{5}{6}$? _____

6. **Writing in Math** The mixed numbers $1\frac{1}{4}$ and $1\frac{2}{5}$ cannot be simplified. Do you need to simplify the answer to $1\frac{1}{4} \times 1\frac{2}{5}$? Explain why or why not.

_____

_____

_____

_____

Understanding Division with Fractions

Quilt Mrs. Bauer's class is making a quilt to donate to a charity. The quilt will be 9 ft wide and 6 ft long. The quilt is being made of squares that are $\frac{1}{4}$ ft long and $\frac{1}{4}$ ft wide.

1. How many squares long will the quilt be? (Hint: The quilt is 6 ft long and each square is $\frac{1}{4}$ ft long.)

   _____

2. How many squares wide will the quilt be? (Hint: The quilt is 9 ft wide and each square is $\frac{1}{4}$ ft wide.)

   _____

3. If each square measured $\frac{1}{3}$ ft by $\frac{1}{3}$ ft, how many squares long and wide would the quilt be?

   _____

Measures A yard is divided into 3 ft. Each foot is divided into 12 in. There are 36 in. in a yard.

4. How many $\frac{1}{3}$ ft segments are there in a yard?   _____

5. How many $\frac{3}{4}$ in. segments are there in a foot?   _____

6. How many $\frac{1}{2}$ in. segments are in a yard?   _____

7. How many $\frac{1}{9}$ ft segments are there in a yard?   _____

8. **Writing in Math** Explain how you found your answer to Exercise 1.

   _____

   _____

   _____

   _____

PROBLEM-SOLVING SKILL
Choose an Operation

Coin Collection Sylvia has a collection of coins from all over the world. She counted her coins and found that she had 35 of them. She also found that $\frac{2}{7}$ of them were from European countries. How many coins were from European countries?

Read and Understand

1. Draw a picture to show the main idea.

2. What are you trying to find?

_____

_____

Plan and Solve

3. What operation will you use? _____

4. Write an equation and solve the problem.

_____

5. Write your answer in a complete sentence.

_____

Look Back and Check

6. Explain how you can check your answer.

_____

_____

Name_____

Baseball Cards

Jeff, Stewart, and Jason traded baseball cards. After the trades, Jeff had 48 cards. He had given 6 cards to Stewart in exchange for 4, and he had given 7 cards to Jason in exchange for 9. How many cards did Jeff have before the trades?

Read and Understand

1. How many cards did Jeff receive from Stewart and Jason?

   _____

2. How many cards did Jeff trade away to Stewart and Jason?

   _____

3. How many cards did Jeff finish with?   _____

4. What are you trying to find?

   _____

Plan and Solve

5. What strategy will you use?   _____

6. Write an equation and solve the problem.

   _____

7. Write your answer in a complete sentence.

   _____

Look Back and Check

8. Is your answer reasonable?

   _____

   _____

Name_____

Customary Units of Length

The drawing below shows the measurements of a professional basketball court.

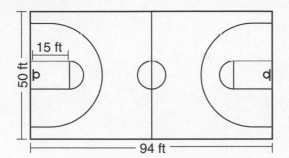

1. How long is a professional basketball court in yards and feet?

_____

2. What is the length of the court in inches?

_____

3. How many inches wide is a professional basketball court?

_____

4. What is the width of the court in yards and feet?

_____

5. How many yards is it from the backboard to the free-throw line?

_____

6. How many inches of floor length are there between the backboard of the hoop and the free-throw line?

_____

7. How many inches is the perimeter of the professional basketball court?

_____

8. How much greater is the length of the basketball court than the width? Write the answer in inches.

_____

9. **Writing in Math** Explain how to convert 4 yd into inches.

_____

_____

_____

Measuring with Fractions of an Inch   PS 9-2

Aneesa is measuring books to see which shelves to put them on. Real books are 4 times taller than the books below. Find the real height of each book.

1.

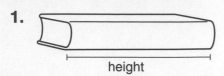

height

_____

2.

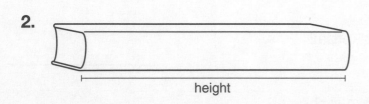

height

_____

3.

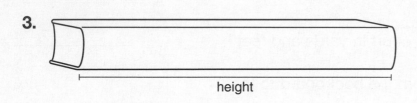

height

_____

4.

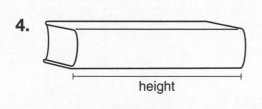

height

_____

5. Writing in Math Explain how you found the height of the book in Exercise 4.

_____

_____

Metric Units of Length

Reasonable Measurements Choose a measurement from the list. Use each measurement once.

> 15 cm
> 1 mm
> 4 m
> 100 km

1. length of a car _____

2. distance between two cities _____

3. thickness of a fingernail _____

4. length of a pencil _____

Which Is Longer? Choose the greater length.

5. 3 m or 325 cm _____

6. 4,200 mm or 5 m _____

7. 6 km or 6,345 m _____

8. 716 cm or 8 m _____

9. 20,000 m or 25 km _____

10. **Writing in Math** Sandra said she is about 5 m tall. Explain if this is reasonable.

_____

_____

_____

Converting Metric Units Using Decimals

Olympic Swimming The chart shows some of the swimming events at the Olympics.

Olympic Swimming Events

50 m	freestyle
200 m	butterfly
100 m	breaststroke
800 m	freestyle
1,500 m	freestyle

Find the distance of the

1. 50 m freestyle in centimeters.   _____

2. 200 m butterfly in dekameters.   _____

3. 100 m breaststroke in decimeters.   _____

4. 800 m freestyle in millimeters.   _____

5. 1,500 m freestyle in kilometers.   _____

Which event has a distance of

6. 2 hm?   _____

7. 150,000 cm?   _____

8. 10 dam?   _____

9. 0.8 km?   _____

10. Writing in Math Explain how to convert 450 mm to meters.

_____

_____

_____

Name_____

Finding Perimeter

1. The perimeter of a square is 24 ft. What is the length of one side? _____

2. What is the perimeter of a rectangle with a length of 8 in. and a width of 6 in.? _____

3. Find the perimeter of a regular hexagon with a side measuring 15 cm. _____

4. If a regular octagon has a perimeter of 96 ft, what is the length of each side? _____

Find the perimeter of each figure.

5. An equilateral triangle with a side measuring 7 m _____

6. A parallelogram with a length of 9 in. and a width of 5 in. _____

7. A regular nonagon with a side measuring 21 ft _____

Find the perimeter of the rectangle with the given dimensions.

8. $l = 12$ mm, $w = 16$ mm _____

9. $l = 41$ cm, $w = 38$ cm _____

10. **Writing in Math** Katie needs to find the dimensions of a rectangle with a perimeter of 18 ft. Explain how she can find the dimensions. List all of the possible whole number lengths and widths.

_____

_____

_____

_____

_____

Name_____

Finding Circumference

U.S. Coins

Coin	Diameter in Inches	Diameter in Millimeters
Penny	0.8	19.0
Nickel	0.8	21.2
Dime	0.7	17.9
Quarter	1.0	24.3
Half-dollar	1.2	30.6
Dollar	1.0	26.5

Find the circumference of each coin to the nearest tenth of an inch. Use 3.14 for π.

1. nickel _____

2. dime _____

3. quarter _____

4. half-dollar _____

Find the circumference of each coin to the nearest tenth of a millimeter. Use 3.14 for π.

5. half-dollar _____   **6.** penny _____

7. quarter _____   **8.** dime _____

9. nickel _____   **10.** dollar _____

11. Writing in Math Explain how to find the circumference of the circle.

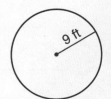
9 ft

_____

_____

Name_____

Finding Area

1. Find the area of the figure.

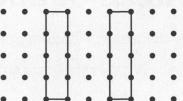

_____

2. Find the area of the figure.

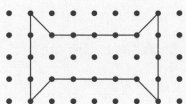

_____

3. Draw a triangle with an area of 8 square units.

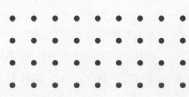

4. Draw a rectangle with an area of 10 square units.

5. Draw a figure with an area of 16 square units.

6. Writing in Math Explain how you found the area of the figure in Exercise 2.

_____

_____

_____

Name_____

Areas of Squares and Rectangles

A diagram of Zachary's garden is shown.

1. What is the perimeter of Zachary's garden?

   _____

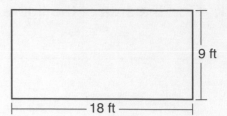
9 ft
18 ft

2. What is the area of Zachary's garden?

   _____

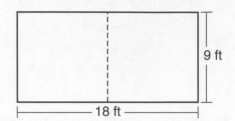
9 ft
18 ft

3. Suppose Zachary divides his garden into two
   equal halves as shown. What are the
   dimensions of each half?   _____

4. What is the perimeter of each half?   _____

5. What is the area of each half?   _____

6. Suppose Zachary divides his garden into four
   equal parts as shown. What are the dimensions
   of each part?

   _____

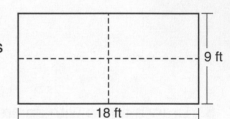
9 ft
18 ft

7. What is the perimeter of each part?   _____

8. What is the area of each part?   _____

9. **Writing in Math** The perimeter of a square is 20 cm.
   Explain how to find the area.

   _____

   _____

   _____

   _____

Areas of Parallelograms

1. Find the area of the parallelogram.

   _____

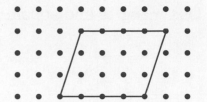

Draw each parallelogram on the dots provided.
Then find the area of each.

2. $b = 5$ units, $h = 3$ units

   _____

3. $b = 6$ units, $h = 2$ units

   _____

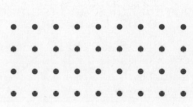

4. $b = 6$ units, $h = 4$ units

   _____

5. **Writing in Math** Is the area of a parallelogram
   with a base of 4 yd and a height of 7 yd greater
   than, less than, or equal to the area of a rectangle
   with a width of 4 yd and a length of 7 yd? Explain.

   _____

   _____

   _____

   _____

Name_____

Areas of Triangles

Use triangles and squares to find the area of each figure.

1.

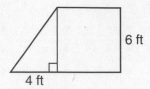

4 m

3 m

_____

2.

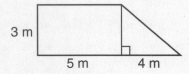

6 ft

4 ft

_____

Use triangles and rectangles to find the area of each figure.

3.

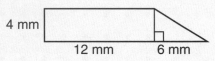

3 m

5 m   4 m

_____

4.

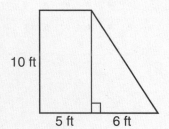

4 mm

12 mm   6 mm

_____

5.

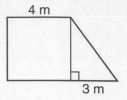

10 ft

5 ft   6 ft

_____

6. Writing in Math Explain how you found the area in Exercise 5.

_____

_____

_____

_____

Name_____

Draw a Picture

Gardening Cara's garden is 12 ft by 8 ft. She wants to plant 4 flowers per square foot. How many flowers will she plant? Draw a picture to solve.

Read and Understand

1. What are the dimensions of Cara's garden?   _____

2. How many flowers will Cara plant per square foot?

   _____

3. What are you trying to find?

   _____

Plan and Solve

4. Draw a picture to help you solve.

5. What is the area of the garden?

   _____

6. How many flowers will Cara plant? Write your answer in a complete sentence.

   _____

Look Back and Check

7. Explain how you can check your answer.

   _____

   _____

   _____

Time

The chart shows the average life span of some animals.

Animal	Average Life Span
Mouse	3 years
Kangaroo	7 years
Pig	10 years
Moose	12 years
Lion	15 years
Bald eagle	40 years
Gray whale	70 years

1. What is the average life span of a mouse in days? _____

2. What is the average life span of a kangaroo in weeks?   _____

3. What is the average life span of a pig in hours?   _____

4. What is the average life span of a moose in weeks?   _____

5. What is the average life span of a lion in days?   _____

6. What is the average life span of a bald eagle in months?   _____

7. What is the average life span of a gray whale in centuries?

_____

8. **Writing in Math** Which is older, a dog that is 83 days old or a cat that is 2,000 hr old? Explain.

_____

_____

Name _____

Elapsed Time

Time Zones There is a 2 hr time difference between cities in the Eastern time zone and cities in the Mountain time zone. If it is 8:00 P.M. in the Eastern time zone, it is 6:00 P.M. in the Mountain time zone. Use the chart to find the length of each flight. The arrival time shown is always the local time.

Flight Schedule

From			To		
City	Time Zone	Departure Time	City	Time Zone	Arrival Time
Miami, FL	Eastern	8:00 A.M.	Santa Fe, NM	Mountain	8:30 A.M.
Denver, CO	Mountain	10:30 A.M.	Boston, MA	Eastern	3:45 P.M.
Portland, ME	Eastern	1:00 P.M.	Helena, MT	Mountain	2:45 P.M.
Norfolk, VA	Eastern	3:30 P.M.	Boulder, CO	Mountain	5:00 P.M.

1. Denver to Boston _____

2. Norfolk to Boulder _____

3. Miami to Santa Fe _____

4. Portland to Helena _____

5. Sumi is flying from Miami to Santa Fe and then back to Miami. How long will she be flying? _____

6. Hector is flying from Norfolk to Boulder and back. Next week he is flying from Portland to Helena and back. How long will he be flying in all? _____

7. **Writing in Math** If it is 10:00 P.M. in Norfolk, VA, what time is it in Santa Fe, NM? Explain.

_____

_____

_____

© Pearson Education, Inc. 5

Use with Lesson 9-13. **129**

Name_____

Temperature

Average Highs Veronica kept track of the average high
temperature in her city for six months. She recorded the
temperatures in degrees Fahrenheit for three months and
in degrees Celsius for three months.

Average Temperatures

Month	Temperature
February	42°F
April	62°F
June	84°F
August	33°C
October	17°C
December	4°C

°F °C

120 50
110 40
100
90 30
80
70 20
60
50 10
40
30 0
20
10 −10
0
−10 −20
−20 −30

Use the thermometer to find the approximate
average high for each month in Celsius.

1. February   **2.** April   **3.** June

_____   _____   _____

4. Find the change in temperature from
February to June.   _____

Use the thermometer to find the approximate average high
for each month in Fahrenheit.

5. August   _____

6. October   _____

7. December   _____

8. Find the change in temperature from
August to December.   _____

9. **Writing in Math** It is 4°C. Is it above or below freezing? Explain.

_____

Name_____

Writing to Explain

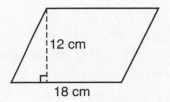

Area Find the area of the parallelogram.
Explain how you found the area.

Read and Understand

1. What is the length of the base?   _____

2. What is the length of the height?   _____

3. What are you trying to find?

_____

Plan and Solve

4. What is the formula for area?

_____

5. What is the area of the parallelogram?

_____

6. Explain how you found the area.

_____

_____

_____

_____

Look Back and Check

7. Explain how you can check your answer.

_____

_____

PROBLEM-SOLVING APPLICATIONS
Fence

Magdalena bought 320 ft of fencing material for her yard. If her yard is three times as long as it is wide, what is the length of her yard? Draw a picture to solve.

Read and Understand

1. How much fencing did Magdalena buy? _____

2. What shape is Magdalena's yard? _____

3. What are you trying to find?

_____

Plan and Solve

4. Is 320 ft the area or perimeter of Magdalena's yard? _____

5. Draw a picture to solve the problem.

6. What is the length? Write your answer in a complete sentence.

_____

Look Back and Check

7. Explain how you can check your answer.

_____

_____

Solve Another Problem

8. Fred's garden is the same width as Frank's but is 2 ft longer. Frank's square garden is 10 ft wide. What is the area of Fred's garden? _____

Name_____

Solid Figures

Wrap It Up Jamie wants to help her mother wrap two presents. The two boxes they will be using are shown.

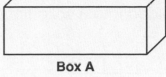

Box A

1. How many faces does each box have?

   _____

Box B

2. Classify Box A as a solid figure.

   _____

3. Classify Box B as a solid figure. _____

4. What is this solid figure?

   _____

5. How many flat surfaces does this solid figure have? What shape are these flat surfaces? _____

6. How many edges does this solid figure have? _____

7. How many vertices does this solid figure have? _____

8. **Writing in Math** Name two objects that resemble a rectangular prism and a cylinder.

   _____

   _____

   _____

   _____

Name_____

Views of Solid Figures

Net or Not? Tell whether each plane figure is a net and can be folded into a solid figure.

1. 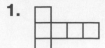 _____

2. _____

3. 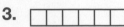 _____

4. _____

5. _____

6. Make a rough sketch of the city block looking directly down from above.

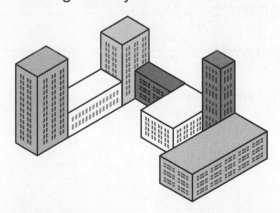

7. **Writing in Math** Name two solid figures that would look the same from the top, side, and front views. Explain.

_____

_____

_____

Surface Area

Woodworking Peter is building a storage chest in woodworking class. To help him plan the project, Peter made the drawing shown.

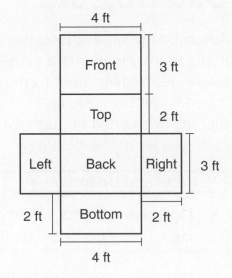

1. What is the surface area of the front section? Which part has the same surface area?

   _____

2. What is the surface area of the top? Which part has the same surface area?

   _____

3. What is the surface area of the right side? Which part has the same surface area?

   _____

4. What is the total surface area of the chest? _____

5. Use the formula for surface area to find the surface area of the figure shown. _____

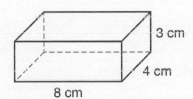

6. **Writing in Math** Explain how you can find the surface area of a cube 2 ft on a side using mental math.

   _____

   _____

   _____

Name_____

Use Objects

Juice Cans Mr. Hanson wants to make a display of juice cans in his store. He wants a single can of juice on the top layer. Every other layer must form a square, with each layer being 1 can wider than the layer above it. The shelf for the juice display is only tall enough for 4 layers of cans. How many cans will be in the display?

Read and Understand

1. How many layers will fit on the shelf?
   How many cans are on the top layer?   _____

2. What are you trying to find?

   _____

Plan and Solve

3. What strategy will you use?   _____

4. Use centimeter cubes to make a model.

5. Solve the problem. Write the answer in a complete sentence.

   _____

   _____

Look Back and Check

6. Is your answer reasonable?

   _____

   _____

Name_____

Volume

A maker of cubic number blocks packs a rectangular box so that there are 8 blocks along one edge, 10 blocks along the second edge, and 4 blocks along the third edge.

1. How many blocks will be shipped in this box? _____

2. If each block has a side of 1.5 cm, what is the volume of the box? _____

3. Another maker of number blocks packs a box so that there are 6 blocks along one edge, 5 blocks along another edge, and 12 blocks along the third edge. These blocks are smaller, however. Each has a side of 1 cm. What is the volume of this box? _____

Kerry bought a new fish tank. The drawing shows the dimensions of the tank.

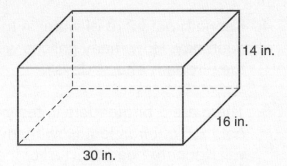

14 in.

16 in.

30 in.

4. What is the volume of the tank?

_____

5. If Kerry fills the tank with 10 in. of water, how much water is in the tank? How much of the tank is empty?

_____

6. **Writing in Math** Two rectangular prisms have the same volume and the same height, even though the length and width of each rectangular prism is different. What do you know about their bases? Explain.

_____

_____

_____

_____

Customary Units of Capacity

Company Hank has some friends coming over and he wants to
serve refreshments. He makes 3 qt of lemonade to serve his guests.

1. How many 12 fl oz glasses will Hank get from
   this pitcher? _____

2. If he has 11 guests coming, will everyone be
   able to have a 12 fl oz glass of lemonade? _____

3. If Hank wants to serve himself and his
   11 guests lemonade, what size glasses
   should he use? Write your answer in cups. _____

Birdfeeders Kenneth helps his grandmother care for the
birdfeeders and birdbath in her yard.

4. Kenneth puts 2 qt of water in the birdbath
   each day. How many gallons will he put in
   the birdbath after 4 days? _____

5. There are 5 birdfeeders in the yard. Each can
   hold 2 c of birdseed. How many pints of seed
   will Kenneth need to fill all of the feeders? _____

6. **Writing in Math** If Kenneth bought a 2 qt container of
   birdseed to fill the feeders, will there be enough? Explain.

   _____

   _____

   _____

   _____

   _____

   _____

Metric Units of Capacity

Shopping Natalie went to the store to buy some bottled water. There is a 1 L bottle for $1.99, a 2 L bottle for $2.99, and a pack of 6 bottles that each contain 354 mL of water for $2.99.

1. How many milliliters of water are in the 1 L bottle?

   _____

2. How many milliliters of water are in the 2 L bottle?

   _____

3. How many milliliters of water are in the pack of 6 bottles?

   _____

4. Which purchase would give Natalie the greatest amount of water?

_____

Warming Up The Johnson family is going sledding. They want to take along some hot cocoa in their thermos. The thermos has a capacity of 1.6 L.

5. To make 200 mL of cocoa, you need 2 scoops of cocoa mix. How many scoops will they need to fill the thermos?

   _____

6. If it takes 236 mL of cocoa to fill 1 c, about how many cups of cocoa will the family get from the filled thermos?

_____

7. **Writing in Math** Explain how you found your answer to Exercise 6.

_____

_____

_____

Customary Units of Weight

Dinner Hank went to the store and bought 1 lb of hamburger and 2 lb of pasta to make dinner for friends.

1. Hank used 10 oz of hamburger for dinner. How many ounces were left? _____

2. He also used $1\frac{1}{2}$ lb of pasta for dinner. How many ounces were left? _____

3. For his next party, Hank ordered a party sandwich. It was 3 ft long and weighed 3 lb. Eleven guests each had a 4 oz piece of the sandwich. How much of the sandwich was left? _____

Truck Mr. Denny drives a truck for the National Stone Company. His truck weighs $1\frac{1}{2}$ T.

4. How many pounds does Mr. Denny's truck weigh? _____

5. A customer orders 22 T of stone. What is the total weight of the truck after the stone is loaded? Give the weight in tons and pounds.

_____

6. **Writing in Math** Explain how you converted the weight of Mr. Denny's truck from tons to pounds.

_____

_____

_____

_____

_____

_____

Metric Units of Mass

Coins The table shows the mass of U.S. coins.

Coin	Value	Mass
Penny	$0.01	3 g
Nickel	$0.05	5 g
Dime	$0.10	2 g
Quarter	$0.25	6 g
Half-dollar	$0.50	11 g

1. Joe has 3 coins that have a total value of $0.25. The coins have a total mass of 9 g. What are the coins?

   _____

2. Fran has some coins that have a total value of $0.80. The coins have a total mass of 32 g. What are the coins?

   _____

3. Suppose you have some coins that have a total mass of 12 g. What is the greatest value the coins could be? What will the coins be? _____

Breakfast Mrs. Hanson bought a box of cereal with a mass of 560 g.

4. What is the mass of the box in milligrams? In kilograms?

   _____

5. If there are 55,000 mg in 1 serving of cereal, about how many servings will Mrs. Hanson's family get from this box? _____

6. **Writing in Math** Explain how you would convert the mass of a dime to milligrams and kilograms.

   _____

   _____

   _____

   _____

Name_____

Exact Answer or Estimate

Field Trip The first-grade classes are going to a pumpkin patch for a field trip. There are 3 first-grade classes. One class has 17 students, one has 18, and another 19. A bus can hold 60 students. Will one bus be enough to transport the students?

Read and Understand

1. How many classes are there? How many students are in each class?

_____

2. How many passengers can one bus transport?   _____

3. What are you trying to find?

_____

Plan and Solve

4. Is an exact answer or estimate needed? Explain.

_____

_____

_____

5. Solve the problem. Write the answer in a complete sentence.

_____

_____

_____

Look Back and Check

6. Is your answer reasonable?

_____

Name_____

Roller Coaster

A roller coaster that opened in 2000 consists of 6,595 ft of track. Trains holding 36 passengers each travel at 92 mph. If the ride can handle 1,600 passengers in 1 hr, about how many trains will travel the track during that time?

Read and Understand

1. How many passengers fit
   in 1 train?   _____

2. How many passengers ride the
   roller coaster in 1 hr?   _____

3. What are you trying to find?

   _____

Plan and Solve

4. Is an exact answer or estimate needed? Explain.

   _____

5. How can you solve the problem?

   _____

   _____

6. Write the answer in a complete sentence.

   _____

Look Back and Check

7. Is your answer reasonable?

   _____

   _____

Understanding Ratios

U.S. States The chart lists the number of the 50 U.S. states that begin with certain letters of the alphabet.

Number of States That Begin with These Letters			
A	4	N	8
C	3	O	3
I	4	V	2
M	8	W	4

1. What is the ratio of the number of states that start with the letter *A* to the total number of states? _____

2. What is the ratio that describes the number of states that start with the letter *N* to the number of states that start with the letter *O*? _____

3. What is the ratio that describes the number of states that start with the letter *V* to the number of states that start with the letter *M*? _____

4. What is the ratio of the number of states that start with the letter *I* to the number of states that do not start with the letter *I*? _____

5. What is the ratio of the total number of states to the number of states that start with the letter *W*? _____

6. **Writing in Math** For Exercise 4, did you write a ratio to compare a part to a part, a part to a whole, or a whole to a part? Explain.

_____

_____

_____

_____

Equal Ratios

Music Store The owner of a music store kept a record of all of the music CDs she sold in one week. She then listed how many of each type of CD she sold.

Number of CDs Sold	
Classical	75
Jazz	100
Rap	250
Rock	300
Pop	400
Total	1,125

1. Write a ratio to show the number of classical CDs compared to the number of jazz CDs the music store sold in one week. Then write an equivalent ratio. _____

2. The store owner said that for every 15 CDs she sells, one CD is classical music. Is she correct? _____

3. What is the ratio of rap CDs sold to rock CDs sold in simplest form? _____

4. For every 15 rock CDs sold, how many pop CDs are sold?

5. What is the ratio of jazz CDs sold to rock CDs sold in simplest form? _____

6. **Writing in Math** Use mental math to find two ratios that are equal to 1:5. Explain how you found your answer.

_____

_____

_____

_____

Graphs of Equal Ratios

Running Laps In physical education class, each student was required to run 3 laps around the track.

1. Complete the table to show the total number of laps run by 1, 2, 3, and 4 students.

Number of students	1	2	3	4
Total number of laps				

2. Graph the ordered pairs from the completed table. Then draw a line to connect the ordered pairs.

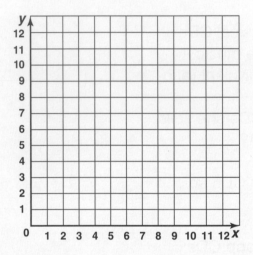

3. If the line on your graph were extended, would the point for (15, 30) be on it? Explain.

_____

_____

_____

4. **Writing in Math** Explain how you can use the graph of a straight line to make a list of equal ratios.

_____

_____

Name _____

Rates

The Heart of the Matter The typical heart rate of a teenager is 70 to 80 beats per minute. The rate is lower during sleep and is higher during exercise.

1. Raul's heart rate went up to 95 beats per minute in physical education class. If he maintained this heart rate for 12 min, how many times did his heart beat in this period? _____

2. If a student counts 300 heartbeats in 4 min, what is his or her heart rate per minute?

_____

Newspaper Delivery Jeff and his sister Lynn work together on a paper route.

3. Each day Jeff delivers 30 newspapers in 1 hr 30 min. Describe the rate at which Jeff delivers newspapers in newspapers per hour.

_____

4. Lynn delivers newspapers at a rate of 45 newspapers per hour. How many newspapers did she deliver today if she worked for 40 min?

_____

5. If Jeff and Lynn ride their bikes on their paper route, they can deliver newspapers at a rate of 50 newspapers per hour. Jeff rode his bike and delivered newspapers for 30 min and Lynn rode her bike and delivered newspapers for 1 hr 30 min. How many newspapers did they deliver altogether?

_____

6. **Writing in Math** Write a sentence that explains why rates always use two different units.

_____

_____

Name_____

Make a Table

Snack Mix Students are preparing a snack mix to take on a hike. In addition to cereal and nuts, the recipe includes 4 tsp of raisins and 3 tsp of sunflower seeds for every 2 servings. The students used 32 tsp of raisins. How many teaspoons of sunflower seeds did they use?

Read and Understand

1. How many teaspoons of raisins are used to prepare 2 servings? How many teaspoons of sunflower seeds?

   _____

2. What are you trying to find?

   _____

Plan and Solve

3. Complete the table to help solve the problem.

Servings								
Raisins								
Sunflower Seeds								

4. Write your answer in a complete sentence.

   _____

Look Back and Check

5. Is your answer reasonable?

   _____

   _____

Scale Drawings

Leaf Study Each member of a fifth-grade class found a leaf to study and draw to scale.

1. One student used a scale of 1 cm = 3 cm for his drawing. If the drawing was 4 cm tall, how tall was the leaf?

   _____

2. A student found a leaf that was 7 in. long. He wanted his scale drawing to be at least 2 in. long but not more than 4 in. long. What scale could he use for his drawing?

   _____

The Eiffel Tower The Eiffel Tower is in Paris, France. It is 986 ft high.

3. If you drew a scale drawing of the Eiffel Tower with a scale of 1 in. = 100 ft, how many inches tall would your drawing be?

   _____

4. Evan needed to draw a scale drawing of the Eiffel Tower that was no more than 4 in. high. What scale could he use to make his drawing?

   _____

5. If you drew a scale drawing of the Eiffel Tower with a scale of 1 cm = 9.86 ft, how many centimeters tall would your scale drawing be?

   _____

6. **Writing in Math** Explain how you found your answer to Exercise 4.

   _____

   _____

PROBLEM-SOLVING SKILL
Writing to Explain

Apples A grocery store counted the number of apples it sold over three time periods. In 20 min it sold 12 apples, in 50 min it sold 25 apples, and in 30 min it sold 13 apples. Predict how many apples the grocery store sells each hour it is open.

Read and Understand

1. How many apples were sold during each time period?

_____

_____

2. What are you trying to find?

_____

_____

Plan and Solve

3. How can you solve the problem?

_____

_____

4. Make a prediction. Write your answer in a complete sentence.

_____

_____

Look Back and Check

5. Is your answer reasonable?

_____

_____

Understanding Percent

Garden Tina planted a garden in her backyard. The drawing shows the types of plants in the garden and the amount of space each type of plant takes up.

Tina's Garden

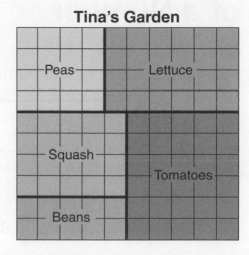

1. Which type of plant takes up 30% of Tina's garden?

   _____

2. Which type of plant takes up less than 15% of Tina's garden?

   _____

3. What percent of the garden has either tomatoes or lettuce?

   _____

4. What percent of the garden is peas?

   _____

5. What percent of the garden is lettuce?

   _____

6. **Writing in Math** Tim said that 50% of the fifth graders and 40% of the sixth graders at his school ride the bus, so he knows that more fifth graders than sixth graders ride the bus. Is he correct? Explain.

   _____

   _____

   _____

Mental Math: Finding a Percent of a Number

State Populations The chart shows information about the populations of the 50 U.S. states.

Population	Percent of U.S. States
Greater than 10,000,000	14%
5,000,000 to 10,000,000	24%
1,000,000 to 4,999,999	46%
Less than 1,000,000	16%

1. How many states have a population greater than 10,000,000? _____

2. How many states have a population less than 5,000,000? _____

3. How many states have a population between 5,000,000 and 10,000,000? _____

Field Trip There were 120 fifth graders who went on a field trip to the science museum.

4. If 10% of the students took part in the insect identification activity, how many students took part? _____

5. If 50% of the students took part in the electricity activity, how many students took part? _____

6. **Writing in Math** Explain how you would use mental math to find 25% of 40.

_____

_____

Estimating Percents

Favorite Fruit Students were surveyed about their favorite fruit. The results are shown in the circle graph. There were 192 students surveyed.

Favorite Fruit

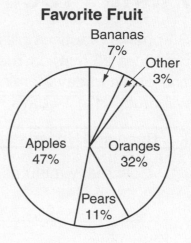

1. About how many students surveyed liked oranges the best?

   _____

2. About how many students surveyed liked apples the best?

   _____

3. Estimate the number of students who liked either bananas or pears the best.

   _____

4. About how much greater is the number of students who liked apples the best than the number of students who liked pears the best?

   _____

5. Estimate the number of students who liked either apples or oranges the best.

   _____

6. **Writing in Math** Use compatible numbers to estimate 39% of 103. Explain how you found your answer.

   _____

   _____

   _____

PROBLEM-SOLVING APPLICATION

Piano Practice

Stephanie practices playing piano each day. On Mondays she
practices 25 min, on Tuesday 32 min, on Wednesday 29 min,
and on Thursday 22 min. Predict how many minutes Stephanie
will practice in 14 days.

Read and Understand

1. How many minutes does Stephanie practice on each of the 4 days?

_____

_____

2. What are you trying to find?

_____

_____

Plan and Solve

3. How can you solve the problem?

_____

_____

4. Make a prediction. Write your answer in a complete sentence.

_____

_____

Look Back and Check

5. Is your answer reasonable?

_____

_____

Name_____

Properties of Equality

Write the missing number that makes each number sentence true.

1. $(2 \times 4) \div 1 = (4 \times 2) \div \square$ _____

2. $(10 \div 5) \times 3 = \square \times 3$ _____

3. $\square + (9 - 3) = 7 + (9 - 3)$ _____

4. $(20 \div 4) - 2 = \square - 2$ _____

5. $(8 \times 6) - 10 = (6 \times 8) - \square$ _____

6. $16 - x = (10 + 6) - \square$ _____

Using the rule given, complete each table.

7.

Rule: Add 25	
34	59
	70
52	77
66	

8.

Rule: Multiply by 7	
13	91
20	140
26	
	217

9. Writing in Math Tina said that if $(3 \times 3) - 5 = (3 \times 3) - n$,
then n must equal 3×3. Is she correct? Explain.

_____

_____

Solving Addition and Subtraction Equations

Use mental math to solve each equation.

1. $a + 18 = 32$ _____

2. $y - 24 = 33$ _____

3. $270 = b + 120$ _____

4. $42 - g = 25$ _____

5. $x + 32 = 75$ _____

6. Altogether, Angela, Toby, and Brian have 508 baseball cards. If Angela has 162 cards and Toby has 139 cards, how many cards does Brian have? _____

7. Michael needs to raise $562 for his trip to Washington, D.C. He earned $275 working at the movie theater. Then he earned $168 selling magazine subscriptions. How much more money does he need? _____

8. Lisa had some CDs. She got 4 more for her birthday. Now she has 36 CDs. How many CDs did Lisa have to begin with? _____

9. **Writing in Math** Jorge had 18 pinecones. He gave some of the pinecones to Martin. Jorge had 11 pinecones left. Explain how to write and solve an equation to find how many pinecones Jorge gave to Martin.

_____

_____

_____

Solving Multiplication and Division Equations

Use mental math to solve each equation.

1. $\frac{n}{2} = 8$ _____

2. $\frac{x}{5} = 5$ _____

3. $\frac{y}{4} = 15$ _____

4. $\frac{b}{10} = 9$ _____

Distance The chart shows the distance each animal could travel in 5 hr if that animal could maintain its top speed.

Cheetah	325 mi
Giraffe	160 mi
Lion	250 mi
Rabbit	175 mi

Find how far each animal can travel in 1 hr.

5. Giraffe _____

6. Cheetah _____

7. Rabbit _____

8. **Writing in Math** Explain how to find how far a lion could travel in 2 hr.

_____

_____

_____

_____

Name_____

Write an Equation

How Far? Angelica lives 27 mi from the lake. If Angelica lives 3 times farther from the lake than Monica, how far does Monica live from the lake?

Read and Understand

1. How far does Angelica live from the lake? How much farther does Angelica live from the lake than Monica?

   _____

2. What are you trying to find?

   _____

   _____

Plan and Solve

3. Write an equation for the problem. _____

4. Solve the problem. Write your answer in a complete sentence.

   _____

Look Back and Check

5. Is your answer reasonable?

   _____

   _____

Solve Another Problem

6. Vance bikes 6 mi per day. How many days will it take him to bike 72 mi? Write an equation to solve the problem.

   _____

Understanding Integers

Temperature The chart shows the temperatures for part of one day.

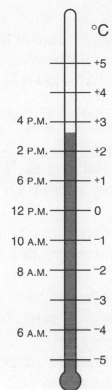

°C

+5
+4
4 P.M. — +3
2 P.M. — +2
6 P.M. — +1
12 P.M. — 0
10 A.M. — −1
8 A.M. — −2
−3
6 A.M. — −4
−5

1. Write the integer that shows the temperature at 6 A.M.

   _____

2. At what time was the temperature one degree below zero?

   _____

3. At what time was the temperature two degrees above zero?

   _____

4. Was it warmer at 10:00 A.M. or 6:00 P.M.?

   _____

5. Was it warmer at 8:00 A.M. or 2:00 P.M.?   _____

6. Gerard had $13. He gave $5 to a friend and spent $3 on a snack. He then found a $5 bill. Order the numbers +13, −5, −3, and +5 from greatest to least.

   _____

7. **Writing in Math** Explain how you found the answer to 6.

   _____

   _____

   _____

Name_____

Adding Integers

Scores Six friends are playing a game using cards. Each time you cannot play at least one card, you score negative points. Right now Paulo has −4 points, Gina +3, Marcus +2, Ivy −1, Xavier +1, and Holly −3. Use the number line for 1–6.

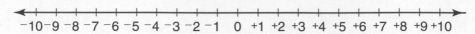

1. If Paulo gets +2 points on his next turn, what will his new score be?   _____

2. If Gina gets −4 points on her next turn, what will her new score be?   _____

3. If Marcus gets −3 points on his next turn, what will his new score be?   _____

4. If Ivy gets +5 points on her next turn, what will her new score be?   _____

5. If Xavier gets −6 points on his next turn, what will his new score be?   _____

6. If Holly gets +6 points on her next turn, what will her new score be?   _____

7. **Writing in Math** Suppose that Paulo and Gina are partners, Marcus and Ivy are partners, and Xavier and Holly are partners. Which pair has the highest combined score? Explain.

    _____

    _____

    _____

    _____

Subtracting Integers

It's Freezing Out Use what you know about subtracting integers to answer 1–7.

1. The temperature is −5°F. What will the temperature be if it drops 10°F? _____

2. When Paulette woke up, the temperature was −1°C. At noon, the temperature was +8°C. How much did the temperature rise? _____

3. It was +10°F. The temperature dropped 12°F. What is the temperature now? _____

4. At 2:00 P.M. the temperature was +14°F. At 8:00 P.M. the temperature was −4°F. How much did the temperature drop? _____

5. At 6:00 P.M. the temperature was +2°C. By 10:00 P.M. the temperature had dropped 5°C. What was the temperature at 10:00 P.M.? _____

6. Alice and Craig were building a snowman. When they started, the temperature was −2°C. By the time they finished, the temperature had dropped 3°C. What was the temperature when they finished building the snowman? _____

7. The temperature is +4°C. What will the temperature be if it drops 7°C? _____

8. **Writing in Math** Petra said that any negative integer minus itself equals zero. Is she correct? Explain.

_____

_____

_____

_____

PROBLEM-SOLVING SKILL   PS 12-8
Writing to Explain

Baby-sitting Hannah earns money by baby-sitting. She earns $7 an hour. For 3 hr of baby-sitting she earns $21, for 4 hr $28, for 5 hr $35, and for 6 hr $42. Explain how the amount of money earned by Hannah changes as the number of hours changes.

Read and Understand

1. How much money does Hannah earn for 1 hr, 3 hr, 4 hr, 5 hr, and 6 hr of baby-sitting?

_____

2. What are you trying to find?

_____

_____

Plan and Solve

3. Identify the quantities shown in the problem.

_____

4. Tell how one quantity changes and the other quantity changes. Write your explanation in a complete sentence.

_____

_____

Look Back and Check

5. Is your answer reasonable?

_____

_____

The Coordinate Plane

Map A coordinate grid illustrating Jake's neighborhood is shown below. Use the map for 1–5.

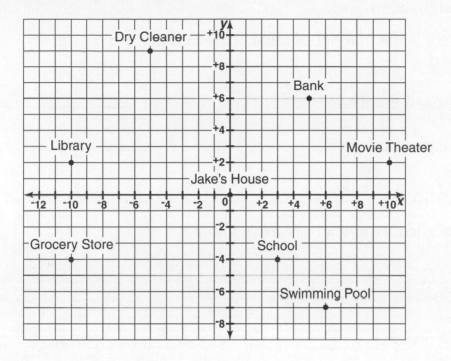

1. What is located at (+3, −4)? _____

2. What is the ordered pair for the location of the grocery store? _____

3. What is located at (−10, +2)? _____

4. What is located at (+6, −7)? _____

5. What is the ordered pair for the location of the movie theater? _____

6. **Writing in Math** Explain how to find the ordered pair for the location of the bank.

_____

_____

_____

Name_____

Graphing Equations

Art Supplies Bonnie and Hector are buying supplies for the art room. Paint brushes cost $2 each, easels cost $9 each, and paint palettes cost $6 each.

Use $y = 2x$, where x is the number of paint brushes and y is the cost, to find

1. the cost of 3 paint brushes. _____

2. the cost of 12 paint brushes. _____

3. the cost of 40 paint brushes. _____

Use $y = 9x$, where x is the number of easels and y is the cost, to find

4. the cost of 2 easels. _____

5. the cost of 13 easels. _____

6. the cost of 100 easels. _____

Use $y = 6x$, where x is the number of paint palettes and y is the cost, to find

7. the cost of 4 paint palettes. _____

8. the cost of 15 paint palettes. _____

9. the cost of 50 paint palettes. _____

10. **Writing in Math** Irene has $95. How many easels can she buy? Explain.

_____

_____

_____

_____

Name_____

Correct!

Jimmy answered 95 math questions correctly. He answered 5 times more questions correctly than Bernie. How many questions did Bernie answer correctly?

Read and Understand

1. How many questions did Jimmy answer correctly? How many more did Jimmy answer correctly than Bernie?

_____

_____

2. What are you trying to find?

_____

_____

Plan and Solve

3. Write an equation for the problem.

_____

4. Solve the problem. Write your answer in a complete sentence.

_____

_____

Look Back and Check

5. Is your answer reasonable?

_____

_____